Praise for *One in Christ*

"Each time I have had the pleasure of spending time with Dr. Ireland I have gained insight into the depth of God's Word, the character of our Savior, and the nature of our Father. A trait I have found in only a handful of others."

—KURT WARNER, NFL Hall of Fame quarterback

"I coach people in the area of money management. Dr. Ireland coaches people in the area of diversity and the development of cross-cultural skills. Having sat under his teaching ministry for years I've watched him masterfully and gently shape a racially diverse audience into a community that has a singular focus—to honor Jesus in how we value each other. Through *One in Christ* he provides one-on-one coaching that will help you improve your effectiveness in the multicultural marketplace and community."

—LYNNETTE KHALFANI-COX, *New York Times* bestselling author, speaker, and personal finance expert

"If you're tired of conversations on culture being high-pitch shouting duologues and yearn for respectful, attentive dialogues; if you want to move conversations on race from hubs of mistrust, huddles of hunches and hammocks of evasions and equivocations; if you want to enter reconciling arenas of action and reconciliation, this is the book for you. It shows in theory and practice how to look at each other with Jesus eyes. David Ireland has written the book we have all been hoping for and waiting on."

—LEONARD SWEET, bestselling author, professor (George Fox University, Drew University, Tabor College), and founder of preachthestory.com

"Sunday morning worship is still the most segregated hour in American society. Only 5 percent of American churches are multiracial. When was the last time you brought a person of another race home for dinner? In his new book, Dr. David Ireland makes the case that diversity begins in our personal lives before it will show up in the church. This book is another tool in your toolbox for twenty-first century ministry!"

—A. R. BERNARD SR., senior pastor, Christian Cultural Center, New York

"David Ireland's new book distills over thirty years of experience building cross-race relationships into a practical guide for others to use. If you feel God is calling you to unite rather than divide and that you need help, *One in Christ* is for you! I have seen Dr. Ireland in action in his own church and I can attest to his authenticity as a reconciler."

—**LUIS PALAU**, international evangelist

"David Ireland's book *One in Christ* is the most profound I have ever read on unity. Ireland embodies the message of his book and powerfully illustrates the life of a reconciler. This is the best catechism available for leading cross culturally."

—**DR. MAC PIER**, CEO and founder, The NYC Leadership Center and co-founder, Movement Day

"Dr. Ireland is a leader who truly embodies the messages he trumpets. His latest book is an important call to unity, as well as a practical how-to manual on achieving it. I recommend this vital message to you as well as its messenger, in hopes that we as a Body move into genuine, biblical friendships, which transcend every area of divide."

—**REV. DR. ROBERT STEARNS**, author of *No, We Can't: Radical Islam, Militant Secularism and the Myth of Coexistence*

"God has given us the greatest commandment: to be in a relationship of love with him and our neighbors. Dr. David Ireland's ministry is a living testimony of this commandment. He has demonstrated that this command of God is real and not just mere words. As we live in a diverse and globalized world today, effectively fulfilling this command through the teachings that he offers, will transform our lives, communities and churches."

—**REV. DR. PAUL CHOI**, president, International Church Planting (InterCP)

"The struggle and tension within people groups has existed from the beginning of time. This struggle continues even today. It is not just an American church struggle; rather it is a global church dilemma. The church birthed on the day of Pentecost is described in Acts 2:8-11 as a church of all people. God's statement in Genesis 11:6 attests to the limitless power of all skins working in harmony. In *One in Christ* Dr. David Ireland takes you on an inner journey of transformation before the outward manifestation. It will challenge you. It will encourage you. It will change you."

—**DR. SAMUEL R. CHAND**, author of *Cracking Your Church's Culture Code* (www.samchand.com)

"God uses David Ireland to communicate His Word with unusual passion and the anointing of the Holy Spirit."

—**PASTOR JIM CYMBALA**, author of *Fresh Wind, Fresh Fire*

"With the depth of wisdom you'd expect from a pastor of over thirty years, Dr. David Ireland shares a wealth of insight on the pressing issue of race relations within America. Where the book shines brightest is in its blueprint for bridging the racial divide. If you are a Christian, the bridge building is your responsibility. Dr. Ireland makes that point crystal clear. You will be challenged and you will be inspired. Most of all, *you will be shown how*. This book is exactly what twenty-first century people need."

—**MICHAEL G. SCALES**, Ed.D., president, Nyack College & Alliance Theological Seminary

"Molding young men into world class athletes occurs on and off the basketball court. I have discovered, however, that skills that make you successful in life are skills that can make you successful on the courts. Dr. Ireland's unique knowledge of how human beings learn to build trust across cultural lines helped coach incoming NBA rookies to develop cross-cultural skills, which helped them to better connect with fellow players. He will coach you in how to better connect with the diverse people in your professional and personal world."

—**PURVIS SHORT**, director, The NBA Rookie Transition Program

"Dr. David Ireland is an amazing apostolic gift with such a prolific mind. His gift is displayed in what he has built and established and maintained. There are those who haven't built anything and cannot teach 'it'. There are those who teach 'it' but haven't built anything. There are those who have built 'it' and can't teach 'it'; but there are those who have built 'it' and teach 'it.' David Ireland has built 'it' and is teaching 'it.'"

—**BISHOP TUDOR BISMARK**, Jabula New Life Ministries, Harare, Zimbabwe

"David Ireland writes in his compelling book, *One in Christ,* that you can't start a meaningful conversation on race with strangers but only with people who trust you. Dr. Ireland can be trusted. He has earned the right to be heard on the topic of racial reconciliation and cross cultural ministry since he writes not as an unproven theorist but as a practitioner, pastor and prophet. *One in Christ* is a critical book for our times."

—**DR. DAN BACKENS**, lead pastor and senior director, New Life Church & One Focus Network

"Dr. David Ireland is extremely gifted at connecting with people across the racial and cultural spectrum. Reading *One in Christ* is a personal opportunity to be coached by him in matters of diversity."

—WILLIE ALFONSO, chaplain, NY Yankees

"These are challenging times in our larger culture. One of these challenges involves the complexity and pain around race and culture—and the division that exists. The Church likes to talk about reconciliation but unfortunately, it has little credibility because it bought into the temptation of segregated churches. In the midst of these tensions and challenges, I'm grateful for leaders like Dr. David Ireland that are seeking to help the Church not only engage the various challenges but to do it from a posture of biblical faithfulness, prayer, and courage. In *One in Christ*, Ireland invites us into this important conversation about building relationships across racial and cultural lines and ultimately, deeper into the heart of God. What a pastoral, prophetic, and practical book!"

—REV. EUGENE CHO, senior pastor (Quest Church) and author of *Overrated: Are We More in Love With the Idea of Changing the World Than Actually Changing the World?*

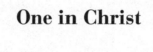

One in Christ

One *in* Christ

BRIDGING RACIAL AND CULTURAL DIVIDES

David D. Ireland, PhD

REGNERY
FAITH

Regnery Faith™ is a trademark of Salem Communications Holding Corporation Regnery® is a registered trademark of Salem Communications Holding Corporation

Unless otherwise indicated, all Scripture herein is from: Holy Bible, New International Version®, NIV® Copyright ©1973, 1978, 1984, 2011 by Biblica, Inc.® Used by permission. All rights reserved worldwide.

Cataloging-in-Publication data on file with the Library of Congress

ISBN 978-1-62157-691-4
e-book ISBN 978-1-62157-710-2

Published in the United States by
Regnery Faith
An imprint of Regnery Publishing
A Division of Salem Media Group
300 New Jersey Ave NW
Washington, DC 20001
www.RegneryFaith.com

Manufactured in the United States of America

10 9 8 7 6 5 4 3 2 1

Books are available in quantity for promotional or premium use. For information on discounts and terms, please visit our website: www.Regnery.com.

This book is lovingly dedicated to the Christ Church congregation. You've taught and encouraged me to stay true to our mission of uniting people to God and people to people.

CONTENTS

Foreword

It is a great honor and privilege to write the foreword to Dr. David Ireland's latest book. All the books he has written have been relevant and helpful. But this book touches the sorest spot in America today—the matter of race. I cannot imagine a book more needed at the present time.

Dr. Ireland has sought to practice what he preaches in this book. I know because I have preached at Christ Church in Rockaway and Montclair, New Jersey many times. He is deeply loved by his flock. I wish all Americans could visit there—not only to hear him preach but to get to know his people. His church is made up of nearly every nationality you can think of.

What David has been doing at Christ Church is what we sought to do at Westminster Chapel, London, over our twenty-five years there. When I first arrived in February 1977 it was almost entirely a white middle class church. I was disturbed by this. I began to pray that Westminster Chapel would "mirror London," that is, reflect the same proportion of people who live in London in our congregation. I wanted the same proportion of Welsh, Nigerians, Indians, English, Pakistanis, Chinese, Kenyans, Scots, South Africans—and even Americans. We largely succeeded. On the final Christmas Day when we met as a congregation for the meal there were twenty-six nationalities present. This so warmed my heart.

I was raised in Kentucky, long known as a "border state" during and after the Civil War. Next door to our house on Hilton Avenue in Ashland was a lovely African American couple, Mr. and Mrs. Laif Scott. Mr. and Mrs. Scott had been slaves and were given their freedom. In those days we referred to them as "colored." Never did we call him by his first name. My father always referred to him as Mr. Scott. That is the way we addressed him. As a consequence of this, I was given a head start in respecting people of different races.

Years later, when we lived in Fort Lauderdale, Florida, I was the pastor of Lauderdale Manors Baptist Church. We were eight blocks from the Mount Olive Baptist Church—a "colored" church that had a gracious pastor. I invited him to preach for us one Sunday evening. He brought his choir along. It was a wonderful evening, unforgettable. It did no harm in bringing us closer and closer to being ONE. But sadly I had members—deacons—who would not attend. And he had members too who would not come along.

What Dr. Ireland has done in his book is to show that the Church should be ONE. Not only that; we have a responsibility to make this happen! This book is not only relevant and timely, but convicting. I pray that the Holy Spirit will deal with all of us through this book— whether we are in leadership or followers in the pews, and whatever our ethnicity. This is a serious matter. I hope that God will speak to you as He has to me in this important book.

—R. T. Kendall, Minister, Westminster Chapel (1977–2002)

Introduction

Picture this, a white guy yelling out the word "alleluia" in the middle of the marketplace in Nairobi, Kenya. You know, that Bible word uttered in every church around the world, which means "the highest praise belongs to God." Somehow it sounds the same in practically every language. Ryan didn't know what else to do but yell *ALLELUIA*. He didn't speak the native Swahili language, only English. As a missionary to Kenya from the States, Ryan was on the mission field there for just a few weeks and was still working through the huge culture shock and bumbling his way through their language.

He had everything he needed to change the flat tire except a jack. What was he to do? That end of the car had to be lifted off the ground to replace the flat tire. Each passerby he stopped just looked at him strangely because of the language barrier and the fact it was weird for them to be accosted by a white guy in Africa. That's when the idea came to him; yell out the word "alleluia." That word, he thought, would summon all genuine Christians to his rescue. They would understand his dilemma. And since they serve the same Master, they would want to help him despite the language, cultural, and racial barriers. It worked. As he yelled, several burly Christian Kenyan men approached him, also saying, "alleluia" each step of the way. In their minds, praise was magnetic. They were drawn to it.

As they approached Ryan, he pointed to the flat tire, still saying *alleluia, alleluia*. They understood. He had a flat tire and was in need of help. He then motioned with his hands, still saying *alleluia, alleluia*, signaling them to lift the rear end of the car so he could remove the flat and put on the spare. Again, they understood and lifted the end of the car he was pointing to. In short order, Ryan had the spare tire on his car. To thank them, he simply said, *alleluia, alleluia*. They did the same, beaming all the while.

As Ryan drove off, he smiled at the remarkable thing that just happened. Though they didn't speak the same language, share the same nationality, culture, or race, they served the same Master. They were all equally committed to fully obeying Jesus and His command to "love your neighbor as yourself." The single word *alleluia* put everything to the test that day. As incredible as this true story is, it points to something equally incredible. We Christians are called by God to model diversity in every area of our lives. In a divided society the church must demonstrate how to model unity. You are the church! I am the church! Together, we must model love for one another despite any external differences we may have.

Humanity: God's Magnum Opus

Humanity is God's highest order of creation. The Bible teaches that God spoke everything into existence *except* humanity. On the first day of creation God said, "Let there be light" and light appeared, making day and night a reality (See Genesis 1:3). On the fifth day God said, "Let the waters teem with living creatures, and let the birds fly above the earth" (v. 20). And it happened without any delay. But when it came to creating humanity, God took a different approach. He didn't speak us into existence. He made us in His image—which means we are designed to reflect God's character of love that embraces all humanity.

To wrap our minds around this distinction we must accept the Bible's use of anthropomorphism—ascribing human qualities to God—so our finite minds can grasp Him. God formed Adam from the dust of the ground with His very hands. This approach is totally different than simply speaking something into existence. It is more personal. It is a hands-on job. This creative approach demonstrates a greater connection to the Creator and the entity being created. God didn't speak us into existence. He handily formed, shaped, and designed us. We are His showpieces, God's magnum opus.

God formed man from the dust of the ground and breathed life into his nostrils. Adam, the first man, became a living soul. Again, using a different but similarly personal approach, God took one of Adam's ribs and from it made a woman. Then Eve, the mother of all humanity, became a living soul.

Because God took such great care in creating human beings, we also must take a careful and personal approach in dealing with each other. This level of care comes into play especially when dealing with people whose racial and cultural backgrounds are unfamiliar to us. Why? Because misunderstandings can easily arise if you lack cross-cultural experience.

Misunderstanding, especially at the onset of any relationship, is the death blow to that budding relationship. That is why you must tread cautiously when learning how to become well-versed in matters of diversity. You're also being careful in light of the fact God has afforded you an awesome opportunity to interface with His magnum opus. The better able you are to relate, communicate, engender trust, and demonstrate mastery across racial and cultural lines, the more opportunities you'll receive from the Lord. Jesus taught when "you have been faithful with a few things; I [God] will put you in charge of many things" (Matthew 25:21). Mastery of diversity leads to additional opportunities to influence more people across racial lines. These opportunities are akin to receiving a promotion.

Promotion is a recurring theme in both the Old and New Testaments. In fact we're told promotion comes from the Lord (Psalm 75:6–7; Matthew 25:21). God wants to promote everyone! He takes a tremendous interest in your advancement. Why? Because when God promotes, He intends to give you an opportunity to deal with His greatest masterpiece—people. A major promotion occurs when you're brought into a role, either personally or professionally, that gives you access not only to more people but also more *kinds* of people. Cross-cultural exposure and positive interracial opportunities reflect a major promotion.

The converse is equally true. An inability to connect with others across racial and cultural lines will lead to fewer opportunities to influence people. Jesus clearly made this point when He said, "For everyone who has will be given more, and he will have an abundance. Whoever does not have, even what he has will be taken from him" (Matthew 25:29). While this may be a tough pill to swallow, we all can appreciate God's wisdom in holding back a promotion from someone who's ineffective. People are important to God, we are His masterpiece, and, if we are unwilling to handle His chief work carefully and delicately, God must place His masterpiece out of reach. Parents, for example, take the same precautions with their priceless heirlooms. If a child is too young, clumsy, or simply unaware of or unwilling to recognize the value of the irreplaceable treasure, it must be placed beyond their reach.

Crossing cultures and building bridges of racial reconciliation becomes easier when you take the approach that people are God's priceless heirloom. When you value people, you value God. When you intentionally learn how to joyfully relate to blacks, whites, Asians, Hispanics, Native Americans, Persians, Pacific Islanders, and all other groups you come in contact with, you're demonstrating greatest appreciation to the Master. You are letting Him know you value His masterpiece. That's why Jesus so quickly declared that after loving God, the very next thing you do to show you have inherited eternal life is to "love your neighbor as yourself" (Luke 10:27). Put another way: you can't say you love the Master if you don't love and value His masterpiece.

My Personal Journey into Diversity

The cliché, "hindsight is 20/20," is true. My passion and personal journey in matters of diversity began thirty years ago. I was twenty-four years old and working bivocationally as an environmental engineer by day and in my other waking moments, as a senior pastor of a newborn, six-member church my wife, Marlinda, and I planted. Having been a Christian just four years, I was so green at pastoring I didn't even know I needed a vision—something so compelling it would attract people to our fledging community and excite them about our future. To complicate matters, Marlinda was expecting our first child and after only two short years of marriage, I was just getting the hang of what it meant to be a husband. Now I was about to enter another major role—fatherhood. I was overwhelmed with life, to say the least.

One evening Marlinda had a taste for something peculiar. I can't even recall now what the unusual combination of food was, but I do recall it sounded weird to me. So, off to the store I went, eager to please my pregnant bride. Once there, I grabbed one of the items on my list. As I placed it in the red hand basket, my eyes glanced to the far end of the aisle. For some odd reason, I noticed the diversity of people shopping. There were African Americans, whites, Latinos, and Asians moving about with their grocery carts. At that moment I heard, for one of the first times in my life, the audible voice of God. It was much like the experience of Samuel when God called to him in 1 Samuel 3. It was so real, as if someone was standing near me shouting my name.

The Lord said to me, "David, why can't it be like that in My house?"

I stood there, frozen for a moment. Then I started to cry.

This was totally not like me. See, I'm not very emotional. In fact, I pride myself on being composed and extremely private with my feelings. Even my closest friends used to call me the Vulcan. If you're a Trekkie you know what that means. One of the lead characters on *Star Trek*, the sci-fi TV program I faithfully watched growing up, is Mr. Spock. He's from the planet Vulcan, which is populated by a race of people who are logical and brainy, but display no emotions. That was me. At least before that moment it was me.

Hearing the voice of God caused me to crumble instantly. I stood there, in the middle of the supermarket, crying uncontrollably. It was as if someone unscrewed the faucet holding my tears back from as far back as I could remember, and I couldn't turn it off. It wasn't just about me hearing the voice of God. This seismic reaction, this sudden inability to hold back my emotions, was because the God of the universe confided in me. Something was of deep concern to Him and He revealed it to me. God was inviting me to help Him address the longstanding problem of prejudice and racial isolation in the church.

The question, "David, why can't it be like that in My house?" was encased in a cultural quagmire that couldn't be unpacked without some thought. God's house was largely monoracial, and He wasn't happy about that. The lack of diversity in the church was—and still is—a huge problem to God. The Lord's question was not merely informational. It was missional. My life's mission would become consumed by the task of addressing this question. God was calling me to become a reconciler. He was assigning me an apostolic mandate to bring diversity to His house. This vision extended beyond my tiny congregation; it is worldwide. Indeed, it was a key aspect of my personal life. I sensed that the more I pursued this mission and worked to improve race relations, God would expand this work far and wide.

Looking back, I was so overwhelmed by this new corporate core value I could hardly finish my shopping. I remember paying for the items as tears streamed down my face. It was an awkward moment for me and the cashier.

Driving home, I was caught in the vortex of my own thoughts. Why did God choose this moment to speak to me? Why couldn't He wait until I was in the privacy of my home? Or better yet, why not wait until I was having my morning devotions? Why did I suddenly develop such a strong burden for diversity? I returned home with more than food for my expectant wife. I returned home with a mission from an expectant God. I shared my experience with Marlinda. My retelling of the story was disjointed, raw with emotion, and hardly coherent, but she too embraced the burden, and we wept over it together.

As God developed this mission in our hearts, we formed a mission statement for our church: "Christ Church exists to unite people to God and people to people." In June 2016 we celebrated thirty years of ministry and now have some 8,500 members, representing over sixty nationalities. Even with this growth, I remain more eager than ever to answer the question God put to me in the supermarket: "David, why can't it be like this in My house?"

Over the years, some of the answers I discovered brought me into various sacred and secular spaces. For a number of years I was a consultant to the National Basketball Association's Rookies Transition Program. Because basketball is an international sport, players have to learn how to get along with team members who are from different races, ethnicities, and nationalities. My assignment was to help players practice diversity off the court so their cross-cultural skills would empower them to be effective on the court.

My experience with the NBA opened the door for other organizations and churches to call on me to help them grow across racial and cultural lines.

I serve as the co-chair of a global, South Korean-based missions organization. Our focus is on reaching people with the gospel of Jesus Christ who reside in the 10/40 Window, a term used to describe the rectangular area of North Africa, the Middle East, and Asia. The countries within this grid are located approximately between 10 and 40 degrees north of the equator. Muslim, Hindu, and Buddhist countries such as Iraq, Vietnam, China, Mongolia, Afghanistan, and Azerbaijan, often called "the resistant belt," lay in the 10/40 Window. This region also has the greatest socioeconomic challenges and the highest resistance to the gospel message.

Our board meeting is held just after our biannual conference, involving some five thousand leaders from sixty-three nations, mostly from the 10/40 Window, who gathered to hear about the work of God around the world. Imagine chairing a meeting with thirty other Christian leaders, each coming from a different country. We were clearly different from one another. Our cultures, ethnicities, races, and even our languages were all different. But we were committed to being together and growing as leaders called to serve our respective nations with the message of Jesus' love and forgiveness.

The anchor languages for our meeting are English and Korean. Each board member, whether from Turkey, Egypt, Uzbekistan, China, or another part of the world, had every part of the meeting translated into his own language. This called for a bilingual Korean translator to be seated next to each member to translate, which required everyone involved to exercise a lot of patience. Chairing this kind of meeting offered me the opportunity to handle God's magnum opus on a high level.

This board position calls for a growing humility on my part because I've been tasked by the Holy Spirit to handle diversity on a global stage. Opportunities like this heighten the unshakeable burden God has placed on my shoulders regarding racial reconciliation and the need to increase the diversity in His house.

The question God posed in that supermarket back in 1984 still gnaws at me to this day. It tugs at my heartstrings. It still keeps me up at night. I can't shake it even when it gets heavy and unattractive. I'm not complaining. I am helping you see how this unusual visitation from the Lord has become a pivotal point in my life. A missional focus and journey began in that supermarket calling for a permanent and irreversible change.

The Book's Aim

This book aims to do three things. First, I want to challenge you to join me in the journey of helping create racially diverse churches. While I'm not suggesting you become a pastor, I am encouraging you to build a diverse life so your friends will follow you to your church. That's how the church will become more diverse. Churches grow mainly because members invite their family and friends. If you have a racially diverse pool of friends, they'll be the people you'll most likely invite to your church. It's as simple as that.

Second, I want to provide you with tools, tested answers that will help you master diversity both personally and professionally. Diversity is science and art. There are some things you can learn to do that will make you more racially attractive. For example, everyone wants to be loved. If you learn how to love people who are different than you, they will grow to trust you. When you earn someone's trust, that person wants to connect with you socially and relationally. The key is learning how to express genuine love to someone who's racially or culturally different from you. This means taking on the mindset of a student. You must learn to love them in a way they can sense and feel. This can be taught.

Third, I will equip you with a biblical framework in which to operate cross-culturally. Jesus was a Jewish carpenter. He looked Jewish and dressed like a first-century Jew, yet He knew how to skillfully cross the racial and cultural divides of His day. The famous story of the Samaritan woman He interacted with at the well is proof positive of His cross-cultural skills (John 4). These skills are transferable once they are outlined in a practical way. In many circles we don't even call ourselves Christians any more. We refer to ourselves as Christ-followers. If that is really the case with you, then you must follow Christ across the racial and cultural divides in your life. You cannot limit following Him to the confines of your race. You must follow Christ wherever and to whomever He goes. That is what it truly means to be an authentic Christ-follower.

We Have Our Orders!

Pastor Stephey Bilynskyj begins each confirmation class with a simple question: "Can you guess how many jelly beans are in this jar?" He takes down each student's answer. Almost immediately he begins another list, this time asking them to name their favorite songs. Now there is a reason behind his questions. With an earned Ph.D. in philosophy from Notre Dame, Bilynskyj was trying to get these students to decide how to answer an even larger question: "When you decide what to believe in terms of your faith, is that more like guessing the number of beans, or more like choosing your favorite song?" The answer is usually the same for old and young alike. They say: "Choosing one's faith is more like choosing a favorite song." Before confirmation is extended Bilynskyj says, "First I try to argue them out of it."[1]

Our culture is charged on both sides of the political aisle on the subject of race. Some are pro diversity while others argue silently or publicly for the separation of races. In some instances the argument has turned into violence. You must choose your favorite song. This choice cannot be based on the allure of a mob or the bias of the media. If you want to be known as "a follower of Jesus" your decision should be influenced solely by Sacred Scripture.

The Bible calls for Christians to be a cross-cultural people. The Great Commission is not optional. Jesus said, you must "Love your neighbor as yourself" (Luke 10:27) and "go make disciples of all nations" (Matthew 28:19). These are cross-cultural mandates we've been commanded to fulfill. You cannot effectively share Christ with a diverse constituency unless you're wielding a cross-cultural savvy when it comes to personal relationships. To some parts of our faith you can choose your favorite song. For example, which church should you attend? The Bible offers guidelines. But at the end of the day, it's your choice. Which political party should you choose? The Bible offers guidelines. But at the end of the day, it's still your choice.

In the matter of diversity, however, God hands you the title of His favorite song and says: I want this to be your favorite song too. Reconciliation must be your favorite song! Reconciliation is everyone's responsibility just like prejudice is everyone's problem.

The fact this book is in your hands demonstrates you care about God's favorite song. You also care about the Great Commission. You care about your personal responsibility to grow as a reconciler. I commend you. May the Lord use *One in Christ* to help you become a true reconciler who labors to bring all of God's people together in Christ.

CHAPTER ONE

Route 316

In the city of Chicago one cold night, a blizzard was setting in. A little boy was selling newspapers on the corner to make a few dollars for food. He walked up to a policeman and said, "Sir, would you happen to know where a poor boy could find a warm place to sleep tonight? I sleep in a box around the corner, and it's too cold to sleep there tonight!"

The policeman looked down at the little boy and said, "Go down the street to that big white house and knock on the door. When they open it just say, John 3:16 and they will let you in."

The little boy left to do as the officer said. He walked to the house, knocked on the door, and a lady answered. He looked up and said, "John 3:16." The lady said, "Come on in, son." She took him in and sat him down in front of a big fireplace and she went off.

One in Christ

He sat there for a while and thought to himself, "John 3:16. I don't understand it, but it sure makes a cold boy warm."

After a while the woman came back and asked, "Are you hungry?"

He said, "Well, just a little. I haven't eaten in a couple of days, and I guess I could stand a little bit of food."

The lady took him in the kitchen and sat him down at a table full of wonderful food. He ate and ate until he couldn't eat anymore. Then he thought to himself, "John 3:16. Boy, I sure don't understand it, but it sure makes a hungry boy full."

She took him upstairs to a bathroom to a huge bathtub filled with warm water. He got in and soaked for a while. As he soaked, he thought to himself, "John 3:16. I sure don't understand it, but it sure makes a dirty boy clean. You know, I've not had a bath, a real bath, for as long as I can remember."

Afterward she tucked him into a large soft bed, pulled the covers up around his neck, kissed him goodnight, and turned out the lights.

As he lay in the darkness and looked out the window at the snow coming down, he thought to himself, "John 3:16. I don't understand it, but it sure makes a tired boy rested."

The next morning after breakfast they sat in front of the fireplace. She took a large Bible and asked the little boy, "Do you understand John 3:16?"

He said, "No, ma'am, I don't. The first time I ever heard it was last night when the police officer told me to use it."

She opened the Bible to John 3:16, and she began to explain to him about Jesus. Right there in front of that huge fireplace, he gave his heart and life to Christ. He sat there and thought, "John 3:16. I don't understand it, but it sure changes everything."[1]

John 3:16 has been called "The gospel in a nutshell," because it summarizes the central message of Jesus. Martin Luther called it "the heart of the Bible, the gospel in miniature." Everything changes when you get a hold of this verse. Or, better said, everything changes when this verse gets a hold of you.

Traveling on Route 316

The words of John 3:16—"For God so loved the world that he gave his one and only Son, that whoever believes in him shall not perish but have eternal life"—were spoken by Jesus to a religious leader named Nicodemus. They formed the centerpiece of their private conversation. Nicodemus latched onto those words and it became the new route on which he would journey through life. The words changed him. They changed his worldview. The words ignited a spark within him, propelling him into a new life—a God kind of life. Nicodemus' world expanded beyond the cultural parameters of his Jewish ethnicity. He became aware that other people existed and they too mattered to God.

To better understand Route 316, you have to better understand Nicodemus. Who is he? What is his background and the circumstances that brought him into the home that night where Jesus was staying? Jesus' words were designed to change the trajectory of this man's life, and they did. Afterward, Nicodemus took another route home—the 316 route.

The Conversation That Changed Everything

John's Gospel paints a wonderful picture of the meeting between Nicodemus and Jesus. The third chapter opens with these words, "Now there was a man of the Pharisees named Nicodemus, a member of the Jewish ruling council. He came to Jesus at night and said, 'Rabbi, we know you are a teacher who has come from God. For no one could perform the miraculous signs you are doing if God were not with him'" (John 3:1–2). When you get a moment, please read the entire chapter. It is fascinating.

In this passage, we recount how Nicodemus came alone to see Jesus under the dark blanket of night. His coming under these circumstances indicate the matter was so personal in nature he didn't want to be spotted by his fellow clerics or questioned by anyone about the reason for his visit. Nicodemus was troubled about his soul. He needed real answers religion was no longer able to provide. Nicodemus had to know if he was in right standing with God. His words convey he knew there was more to life than simply being a doer of the Law. Living merely to obey the Law was not fulfilling. It was empty, heavy, and devoid of a true relationship with God. But he didn't know what to do. Prior to conversation, he saw Jesus only as a "teacher who has come from God." Yet there was something special about this controversial rabbi that led him to seek a private audience.

To understand how significant this meeting was, you must understand Nicodemus' standing in the Jewish community of that time. Nicodemus was a powerful man, a ruler among the Jews. He was one of seventy-two men who made up the Sanhedrin. This council presided over civil problems, matters concerning religious scholarship, and criminal justice issues. The council even had its own police force.

Despite this, Jesus didn't pull any punches. He answered Nicodemus point blank: "Very truly I tell you, no one can see the kingdom of God unless they are born again" (John 3:3). In other words, he needed to have a genuine conversion experience with God. This experience would change him from the inside out. The change was not brought on by another religious class or more education. The Holy Spirit would convict him of his sin, and he would respond with a cry of repentance—a cry for God's mercy. Repentance occurs when you reverse your behavior so it comes into alignment with God's desires.

One of the early church fathers, John Chrysostom, said, "Repentance is a medicine which destroys sin, a gift bestowed from heaven, an admirable virtue, a grace exceeding the power of laws."[2] Jesus was very clear when He called Nicodemus to repentance. He was not going to ignore the fact Nicodemus had gaps in his religious knowledge. That's exactly why Jesus asked, "You are Israel's teacher, and do you not understand these things?" (John 3:10)

Jesus' question was intended to dislodge Nicodemus from his normal religious hiding place. Pharisees had a reputation of being sticklers of the Law. They were widely known as lawdoers. So Jesus did not want Nicodemus to leave His company that night with the idea of "more laws and more rules." Instead He wanted this man to understand God's amazing love toward him and all people. So when Jesus spoke the words, "For God so loved the world...," Nicodemus had no choice but to surrender to a fresh revelation of God. He was forced to see God as generous, big-hearted, and selfless. God's love is redemptive. It rescues people from their sinfulness. Nicodemus also learned

God's love is personal. At the same time, he discovered God's love included everybody, everywhere in the whole world.

As a first-century Jew, Nicodemus only knew of the usual Jewish refrain, "God loves Israel." The rabbis he studied under and walked with didn't teach God loves the world. They only referenced God's love for Israel. Hearing these words from the lips of Jesus was groundbreaking. The reality of God's love being generous enough to embrace the whole world was not only unconventional; it was radical.

I can imagine as Nicodemus processed this revolutionary idea, it dawned on him God loves all humanity, even the Gentiles. This truth did not negate the reality of God's love for the Jews. It simply emphasized that both realities must coexist with equal attention, assertion, and practice. Route 316 living calls us to love people beyond the borders of our own race, ethnicity, and culture. If we truly have experienced salvation, our love for people—all kinds of people—will confirm our born-again experience.

Nicodemus was a Pharisee. The word means "separated ones." They lived within cloistered communities so they would not be defiled by sinners—anyone who was not like them, especially Gentiles. Pharisees were legalists who reeked of self-righteousness. They were consumed by rules and performing religious rituals, including fasting, closely following a kosher diet, circumcision, and strict Sabbath observance.

Nicodemus, like most Pharisees, could not see how his self-righteous and judgmental ways hindered others from relating to him or seeing the heart of God. He couldn't see how his smugly moralistic intolerance toward others—their opinions, behavior, and differences—was sin. He needed repentance to bring him into a genuine relationship with God. This change would also open a wide door of social opportunities—the kind that would bring him into social circles with other people beyond the ranks of his own small community. This would eradicate the usual awkwardness and discomfort he felt because of his previous monocultural living. It opened a new worldview to Nicodemus.

Prior to hearing the 316 challenge, Nicodemus, like most first-century Jews, expected Jesus to hold to the same view of other races as he held. He believed everything he needed to live a complete and satisfying life could be found within the borders of his own ethnicity. Jesus dismantled that premise.

A surprising reality is that Jesus is doing the same thing today. The church is largely monoracial because Christians are uncomfortable with people who don't look like them. Anyone who thinks a fulfilled life is a monoracial or monocultural life is sadly mistaken. A fulfilled life is a racially diverse life. A fulfilled life occurs on Route 316. God loves the world and you must too. Personal fulfillment starts there. Jesus made this fact very plain to Nicodemus as He confronted him that evening. And He must make it very plain to you, too.

Jesus Lovingly Confronts Us

No one likes to be confronted. I hate when my wife says to me, "We need to talk." It doesn't matter how sweetly she says it or if she calls me "Honey" when she says it. Even if she's smiling while the words drip from her lips, I don't like hearing those four words: "We need to talk." They tell me I'm going to be confronted about something. Having heard those words many times in our thirty-three years of marriage, they still cause me a little uneasiness. Yet looking back over the years, I attribute the health of our marriage to those "we need to talk" discussions. Whether initiated by me or by Marlinda, the confrontation was always necessary and, thankfully, always ended on a positive note.

When your confronter has your best interest at heart, confrontation is positive. It's negative when his aim is to embarrass, poke at, put down, or demean you. Run from those kinds of confronters. Mark Twain warns, "Keep away from people who try to belittle your ambitions. Small people always do that, but the really great make you feel that you, too, can become great."[3] Similarly, the kind of person Ralph Waldo Emerson says will be of benefit is, "someone who will make me do what I can."[4]

When Jesus confronted Nicodemus, there was never a hint of embarrassment, shaming, or any attempt to condemn his previous perspective, though it was quite limiting. Jesus' confrontation was only aimed at having Nicodemus do what he could do. He could become stronger, better, and more equipped to succeed in the multicultural world. Any confrontation by the Holy Spirit you experience will produce the same results, but you have to be open to the confrontation and be willing to allow it to change you.

There's no doubt Jesus' approach is impressive. He spoke the truth in love. He confronted the erring scholar with panache, style, and charm, but we must not lose sight of Nicodemus' response. He accepted the confrontation. He didn't run out of the house covering his ears. He allowed the confrontation, as uncomfortable as it may have been, to change him.

In his book, *Beliefs, Attitudes and Values*, Milton Rokeach, a behavioral scientist, points to an important observation: personal change occurs because of two kinds of stimuli. First, people change when they are constantly confronted with social and societal pressure; it becomes overwhelming and unavoidable.[5] Second, people change when they're confronted with their own personal values and conscience and their actions don't align with their beliefs. The hypocrisy of their own life troubles them to the point that it induces change.

We must conclude that confrontation occurs on one of two levels. It either emanates externally from an outside source or surfaces internally from personal conviction of one's own conscience. Regardless of the source or the starting point, conviction leads to personal change.

External Confrontation

I used to tell one of the members in my church, Joey (pseudonym), that his perspective was too limited. It needed to be broadened to become more inclusive. Joey was a nice guy and a godly man, but his lifestyle was largely monocultural. He couldn't see he was living a racially and culturally isolated life. Being a member of a church that was racially and culturally diverse gave him the illusion he was a multicultural guy. In reality he was physically present but emotionally and socially absent from the diversity aspect of our congregation. He didn't contribute to our diversity. He didn't have friends of different races and he didn't see his social isolation was indicative of a deeper problem. Much like Nicodemus before his confrontation from Jesus, Joey was happy traveling along the monocultural highway. That's the only thing he knew. That was the only life he was aware he could have.

Once, when I accepted a speaking engagement in Germany, I invited Joey along. He was so excited. Born in a small city in New Jersey, Joey never lived more than thirty miles from Hackensack—except when he attended college in upstate New York. For the first time in his life this thirty-five-year-old man held a passport. That's not so odd because some 70 percent of Americans don't own a passport, according to the State Department.[6] But though you may be limited in your travels to other countries, that is no reason for you to remain limited cross-culturally. And I must make this point! Jesus never traveled more than two hundred miles from His birthplace yet He wrote the book on diversity. Diversity begins in the heart and not in the airport or overseas, but sometimes travel helps to open our eyes and confront us about our shallowness.

Joey was like a kid in a candy factory while at the airport. He stared at everything. When we landed in Germany, he was like a sponge. When my German host asked him, "Where are you from?" Joey, deciphering his broken English, answered, "Hackensack." The host looked at him with this quizzical look. His eyes were asking for clarity, for more information, for a global context. I jumped in and said, "New York—a little town outside New York City." When you're overseas the answer to the question of where you live is New York, for us who live in New Jersey. Even our airport, "Newark Airport," goes by the name, "Newark-New York" when you see it appear on the destination screens while overseas.

My host smiled when he heard New York because he now had a mental picture of where Joey was from. He had context—a cultural and global context. When we got back to the hotel, Joey asked me, "What was that exchange all about? You know, your answer of where I live. I don't live in New York. I live in Hackensack." This was my opportunity to lovingly confront Joey's limited perspective. "Joey, Andreas lives on the other side of the Atlantic Ocean on a different continent," I said. "Do you think he's ever heard of the tiny city of Hackensack, New Jersey?" Before I gave him a chance to answer I continued, "A lot of people living in New Jersey have never even heard of Hackensack."

Joey's eyes opened to the smallness of his perspective. This geography lesson and the context required to answer someone's question who resides on a different continent, in a different nation, and with a different culture and language, opened Joey's eyes. Joey was confronted externally by the fact he had to put himself in Andreas' shoes to help him understand how to answer the question. External confrontation is never without its discomfort. Some of us need that to get redirected to Route 316—the right road to the God kind of life.

Confrontation Can Be Public

Confrontation of your perspectives sometimes has to be public in order for you to see yourself, or at least how you're coming across to others. I was shocked alongside many other Americans who tuned in to *Good Morning America* to see a news story on a fifty-two-year-old man wearing a pair of short shorts—the kind Daisy Duke wore in the old sitcom *The Dukes of Hazzard*. They were tight, extremely short, revealing, and embarrassing, to say the least.

This dad was tired of having his nineteen-year-old daughter, Myley, ignore his paternal advice to dress modestly. She, like so many other teenage girls, favored skimpy clothes to show off her newfound womanly curves. In her effort to look "hot" she found nothing wrong with the long seductive stares she drew from guys who undressed her with their eyes.

Myley hadn't been buying her dad's lessons on how modesty safeguards her worth as a young lady. So he used a different method to convey the same truth. He came out of character. He went public with his confrontation. His words were falling on deaf ears. So he chose to silently, yet publicly confront her. He was no longer the conservative, modest father who dressed his age. Instead, he cut off the legs of a pair of old jeans and turned them into his own Daisy Duke shorts. The entire family was speechless when dad donned these skintight jeans that revealed parts of his anatomy that were almost illegal to show in public.

He even kept them on when they played miniature golf at the public course. Strangers pointed, stared, and snickered, as did his daughter. And then, to get an even bigger laugh, she posted a picture of him wearing his short shorts on one of her social media sites. To her surprise, the photo went viral. Overnight it received more than 130,000 comments, drawing the attention of media outlets, which led to *Good Morning America* requesting an interview with the family.

The dad's behavior made a lasting impression on Myley. Her takeaway, when asked by the reporter, was to say she'd learned her lesson. "It got the point across," she said.[7]

When people's racial and cultural behavior is hard for them to see, public confrontation is essential to opening their eyes to their racial and cultural myopia. It has to be handled delicately though. Myley's picture of her dad wearing those ridiculous shorts was indelibly etched in her mind. That is what public confrontation is supposed to do. You're forced to see yourself in a new light. Admittedly, it can be painful.

Learning your once-held view of prejudice is never enjoyable. Even if your view of racial separation stems from ignorance, lack of awareness, or practices of your family of origin, you must abandon it if you're going to live as a fully devoted disciple of Jesus Christ. You cannot fulfill the Great Commission if there is even an iota of thought in your mind that says: "You stay over there in your racial space, and I'll stay over here in mine." Racial isolation is a cancer to the call of God to walk in unity.

Confrontation Is Necessary

In May 2017, I went to South Korea for a speaking engagement. One of the South Korean speakers admitted that his nation is facing a major dilemma regarding diversity. Korea is largely monoracial. But now, due to trade, tourism, the attraction of foreign students to its universities, and Korea's rise in international business, the nation is slowly approaching a demographic picture showing 10 percent of the nation will soon be non-Korean. "We will need help in becoming multicultural," the speaker confessed. This observation was made because problems involving race relations are on the rise and the need for external confrontation is steadily increasing along with it.

Although external confrontation may help to stimulate change in how you view people, the likelihood of you changing only becomes a reality when you trust the confronter. The confronter must have a basis for speaking to your life. Relational authority is the only platform a confronter can legitimately speak from when the aim is to get you onto Route 316.

In March 2015 Starbucks launched a broad initiative intended to help improve race relations in America. They called it Race Together.[8] The campaign's aim was to help facilitate a national conversation on race relations with the hope of helping Americans take steps toward getting along better with one another. Starbucks baristas were instructed to write the words: "Race Together" on the purchaser's coffee cup before delivering the drink. Baristas were also tasked to initiate conversations on race through a series of conversation starters.

The whole initiative flopped. Some people laughed. Others mocked. The late-night talk show hosts got a lot of free fodder, thanks to Starbucks' ignorance concerning race relations.

There were a myriad of reasons for the failure. First, Starbucks had its own diversity problems. But the most pronounced reason for the campaign's shortcomings was the failure of the company to recognize you can't start a conversation on race with strangers. You haven't earned their trust and they haven't given you permission to enter that private part of their world. The success of external confrontation rises and falls on the relational connection you have with the person being confronted. If you're going to confront someone, begin by earning that right by building a relationship with him or her. Relationship is the currency in external confrontation.

It may not take long to establish an authentic relationship. The key, however, is that it must be authentic and sincere. Jesus didn't have a longstanding relationship with Nicodemus. Certainly, Nicodemus knew who He was and could have attended some of Jesus' sermons. But he didn't have a long history of knowing the Savior. The fact that Jesus said to Nicodemus, "You are Israel's teacher," is an indicator Jesus had some knowledge of who he was, though. When the external confrontation occurred, Jesus' words erupted in Nicodemus' soul. No one had ever challenged him like that before. His views about God's love toward non-Jews were shattered in that moment. The next thing Nicodemus knew, he was on the onramp of Route 316.

Internal Confrontation

Many things can trigger internal confrontation, but a primary tool used by the Holy Spirit to get us to change is truth. People are brought to repentance and personal change when they experience internal confrontation with truth. Paul says God uses the foolishness of preaching to save people (1 Corinthians 1:21). Preaching contains truth—information that stirs the hearer to give thought and consideration to what he heard. Once the cycle of reasoning has run its course in someone's heart he then decides to change. That cycle cannot be completed until the person comes face-to-face with the discrepancy between what he believes and how he is living. This disjointed state of the heart is where conviction lies. At this point, hypocrisy is seen in one's own heart, positioning it for change.

Internal confrontation is about looking in the mirror of your soul only to be disappointed, angry, or troubled about the person staring back at you. Your own conscience stirs you to change because your conscience attests to your misalignment. You claim to believe the Bible implicitly, yet a critical aspect of your life says otherwise. If Route 316 is your life's highway, you cannot be joyfully riding on some monocultural road all the while claiming to be this ardent Christ-follower. That reflects a misaligned life.

One in Christ

The apostle James paints a clear picture of internal confrontation when he says, "Don't fool yourself into thinking that you are a listener when you are anything but, letting the Word go in one ear and out the other. Act on what you hear! Those who hear and don't act are like those who glance in the mirror, walk away, and two minutes later have no idea who they are, what they look like" (James 1:22–24).

James explains the Word helps us take notice of our disjointed value system when necessary. After hearing God's Word on a matter, whether spoken by a preacher or by someone simply declaring a universal truth such as justice or love for humanity, your conscience becomes awakened to the presence of hypocrisy and change occurs.

There is no prescribed amount of time for conviction to ripen. It's not like baking a cake, with the recipe instructing you to place the prepared batter in the oven at 400 degrees Fahrenheit for forty minutes. Conviction of sin or the need to turn onto Route 316 can either happen immediately or over the course of many years. It all depends on your sensitivity to the Holy Spirit, your regard for the Word, and your awareness of the value of God's magnum opus—people.

A friend of mine who happens to be a white American was visiting China on a mission trip. After a week or so, Chen (pseudonym), one of the Chinese leaders of the underground church, took Michael aside for a personal chat. With tears in his eyes Chen said, "We Chinese leaders have no problem being imprisoned or even becoming martyrs for our faith. We get that. But would you help me learn how to become multicultural? China is largely monoracial. I have no experience interacting with people who are different from me. Can you help me because I want to go on the mission field?"

I was shocked when Michael told me about that exchange. Apparently, Chen had been convicted concerning his shortsightedness regarding other cultures and races. The Holy Spirit had somehow held up a mirror to his soul and he did not look away, pretending everything was all right. He acquiesced to his ignorance and to his tangible need to enter Route 316. If Chen could experience internal conviction while being so far removed from a diverse culture, we living here in the States have absolutely no excuse.

I mentioned that God uses the agency of truth to appeal to our consciences. Sometimes I try to induce internal conviction by getting under people's skin with provocative questions on matters of race. I realize I can't change anyone, but my questions can stimulate deep thought that will bring about internal conviction. One question that has garnered a lot of attention is, "What was the racial composition of your wedding?" I ask this question in classes or seminars I hold on diversity. To include singles in the exercise, I frame the question differently: "Based on your current set of friends, if you were to get married to someone of your race, what would the racial composition of your wedding be?"

I press the issue further by giving some stats about average weddings. There are typically one hundred guests at an average wedding. I then create a table with one column listing the more widely used categories of races—whites, African Americans, Hispanics, Asians, and other. The corresponding column is blank. Each person is asked to take a couple of minutes and fill in the table. "Be honest," I bark.

One in Christ

The people who usually get invited to weddings are family members, close friends, and colleagues of both the bride and the groom. The guests represent the people who play an important relational role in your lives. You want them to witness your special day. Your wedding will be meaningful to them.

If, on your special day, you look across the congregation at the sea of faces and all of them are from the same race—your race, it doesn't matter what excuse or reason you use to defend your invitation list, the facts speak for themselves. You are not as diverse as you think you are. I'm not suggesting you should get rid of your current family and friends. What I'm strongly suggesting is the need to *add* to your pool of friends. Cross-cultural growth will be reflected in your social circle. Period.

After that exercise, I quickly follow up with another question that's equally as disturbing if the numbers don't add up: If you were looking over the walls of heaven on your funeral, what would be the racial composition of the congregation, assuming your current set of friends were the sole guests? This question gets the room buzzing with chatter. Like it or not, those who attend funeral services are the closest people to the deceased. If strangers are present at a funeral, this usually means they felt pity and empathy for the departed. Most likely this empathy is brought on by the fact the person had no living relatives or other caring people in his or her life. This is an anomaly. The guests at funerals are more likely the friends and relatives of the departed.

I usually repeat the question so the subterranean juices of those seeking to take Route 316 can really get flowing. I call for each participant to complete a similar racial information table as the one he or she completed for wedding guests. This table also features two columns—one citing the five demographic categories I listed above and the other is blank. The journeyers fill in the blank spots. Some do it gladly in anticipation of a diverse list. Others leave it blank or cover their table so no one can see that most of the racial categories are blank. The fact they hide their answer sheet is proof positive that internal conviction is at work and change is imminent. That's exactly what I wanted. Internal conviction has been stimulated. Wonderful!

The Benefits of Confrontation

Regardless which method of confrontation is at work in you— the external or internal type—confrontation has terrific benefits. Confrontation challenges your beliefs and values and you benefit by becoming more far-reaching in your ability to deal with people. Confrontation also challenges your character and personal style. Don't shy away from it because you benefit by becoming stronger, more godly in your character, and more competent in interacting with a diverse group of people. Confrontation often challenges your goals and motivation. Yield to it, and you'll experience the benefit of becoming more focused, relevant, and accomplished. After all, if people are God's magnum opus, you want to excel at handling them.

That evening, after his secret conversation with Jesus, I imagine Nicodemus returned home by a new route—the 316 route. He gained a new worldview—a global one. He welcomed confrontation and greatly benefited by it. Do the same and watch the outcome. You will certainly be the better for it.

CHAPTER TWO

Crossing Cultures

On a recent mission trip to Kenya, one of the guys in my group bought a whole set of multilingual gospel coins before leaving the States. These are gold plated coins about 1.5 inches in diameter. John 3:16 is inscribed on one side, and on the flip side is a prayer requesting forgiveness and salvation. When a person receives this coin, the hope is he or she gets saved by reading the Bible verse and then praying the sinner's prayer. Fred (a pseudonym) was intent on using these coins to share his faith, particularly as he came across internationals in the airports. He was not going to allow any language barrier to hinder him from sharing his faith.

If he heard someone speaking Italian, German, or another foreign language of which he could decipher a few words, he'd give them a gospel coin matching their language. Since there are no direct flights from New Jersey to Nairobi, Kenya, we had to connect in Amsterdam's Airport Schiphol, one of Europe's key international airports. We had a three-hour layover there, so as soon as the plane landed at Airport Schiphol, Fred took off through the airport to distribute his gospel coins.

After about an hour, he returned to the gate where the rest of us were sitting, chatting away about our trip. "I have one more gospel coin left," Fred said. "It's in French. I'm going to look for a Frenchman and give him this coin." And off he went again. Fred returned about fifteen minutes later, grinning from ear to ear. Mission accomplished! A Frenchman received the gospel coin.

You Must Be Intentional!

To bridge cultural gaps, you must be intentional. Fred didn't sit around hoping he'd run into someone who was French or Russian or some other nationality that would fit the language of his coins. He prayed, he planned, he was purposeful, and he was proactive. This is what's required if you're going to make a lifestyle shift to model diversity. The only difference, and it's a huge difference, between what Fred did versus what you must do is the need to form relationships with others, and not merely to conduct a transaction.

Fred's behavior was strictly transactional. He was in an international airport for a few hours. He bought gospel coins for the sole purpose of distributing them to foreigners who didn't speak English. Everyone in the airport, with the exception of the workers, was in transit from one country to another. There was no time to form meaningful relationships. Fred only had enough time to distribute the gospel coins. After that, he had to trust the Holy Spirit would use the coins to move people Godward. Fred had to be transactional in his behavior, but that won't work if you're looking to form multicultural friendships.

First, you should avoid anything and everything that speaks of tokenism. That's when you say to yourself, "I need a black friend," "I need a white friend," or a friend of any certain ethnic group. That's wrong. No one would want to befriend you under those terms. Neither should you go about searching for a cross-race friend the way you'd shop for a new dry cleaner. That's transactional. It's wrong because it's devoid of love, care, and authenticity—three vital ingredients to forming healthy cross-race relationships. What you can take away from Fred's actions are his *awareness* of the value of other cultures and his *ownership* of the God-given mandate to cross cultures.

Show Awareness

Crossing cultures requires awareness and intentionality. People who are different from you are—different. Not in their needs but in their cultural distinctions. All human beings share the common need for food, shelter, opportunity, and love. The way we communicate those needs and interface with those within our respective communities reflects the distinction of culture. H. Richard Niebuhr, in his classic book *Christ and Culture*, defines culture as, "The work of men's minds and hands. It is that portion of man's heritage in any place or time which has been given designedly and laboriously by other men. Hence, it includes speech, education, tradition, myth, science, art, philosophy, government, law, rite, beliefs, inventions, technologies."[1]

I was recently in Spain and I quickly learned the cultural norm of kissing someone on both cheeks as a form of greeting. One week later, I was in South Korea. There was no kissing when you greeted someone, rather we had to bow. If you didn't bow you were not only being unsociable, but you were also being blatantly dishonorable. I had to immediately fall in line with both cultural norms and expectations.

Culture frames a large part of your views on social behavior. The difference in one culture versus another is not a bad or a negative thing. It simply requires us to have awareness and understanding of one another's culture. This is a key ingredient in forming meaningful relationships across our cultures. A person who is considered *cross-cultural* is someone who is both comfortable and skillful in living socially in cultures beyond his own. The term *multicultural* means many cultures coexisting together in a larger culture.[2] A multicultural worldview or church is simply one that operates under this principle: people matter to God and they matter to me too. Based on that worldview you demonstrate awareness of the multiple cultures in your midst and you learn to function and joyfully live with them.

The Bible Calls You to Cross Cultures

To build friendships across racial and cultural lines, you must exhibit an understanding that cultures differ, but that God has called you to be cross-cultural. The Great Commission clearly states, "Therefore go and make disciples of all *nations*, baptizing them in the name of the Father and of the Son and of the Holy Spirit" (Matthew 28:19, italics mine). Since the New Testament was originally written in Greek, we must return to that language to fully understand the rich meaning of the English words the translators selected.

The word *nation* is the Greek word *ethnos*, where we get the word *ethnic*. Jesus commissioned us to share the gospel everywhere and across every ethnic line. God wants an ethnically, culturally, and racially diverse family everywhere people exist. We must demonstrate an awareness of this final assignment, referred to as the Great Commission, in how we intentionally choose to live.

The high number of monoracial churches scattered across the American landscape today demonstrates we are either blatantly disobedient to Jesus' final commission or we just don't know how to build multicultural churches. I think it's a bit of both.

The church is made up of people. The local and the universal church cannot attain a multicultural status unless its individual members develop multicultural lives and friendships. Unlike a public school or a business, the church is a member-based organization. There are laws on our books requiring schools to provide equal access to students and faculty across the racial and cultural spectrum. A church does not and cannot legally mandate its members to bring in people from other racial groups underrepresented in its membership. Diversity is a personal choice.

The Great Commission is not a threat or an action we're forced to take. Rather, it is the final wish of our Lord for us to fulfill while we're here on the earth. He spoke the words of Matthew 28:19 in love and love is the vehicle we must employ to complete it.

Loving people who are different from you is a personal choice. Jesus taught us to "love your neighbor as yourself" (Luke 10:27). This is not mandatory, but it is intentional. Jesus would never give us an assignment we're wholly incapable of completing. That would create constant disillusionment and discouragement on our part. A cross-cultural church begins with a cross-cultural life. A cross-cultural life begins when you personally choose to demonstrate awareness of others in a personal way. Their value and significance to God and to you is on display and you're open about it.

The first-century church at Antioch was a multicultural church. In Acts 11:19–26 we discover how it began and how it maintained its rich diversity. Some of the disciples who fled the persecution in Jerusalem wound up in Antioch, three hundred miles away. A port city less than twenty miles from the Mediterranean Sea in Syria, Antioch was a major city of commerce in the Roman Empire that attracted a racially, ethnically, and culturally diverse group of people.

While a number of the Jewish believers fleeing persecution shared their faith only with other Jews, "Some of them, however, men from Cyprus and Cyrene, went to Antioch and began to speak to Greeks also, telling them the good news about the Lord Jesus" (Acts 11:20). This second category of believers was intentional about being diverse. They showed awareness of the Great Commission and their responsibility to live it out in their generation.

These cross-cultural believers were not more skillful in the Scriptures than their monoracial counterparts, they just had a heart for *all* people. They probably reasoned, "Doesn't Christ care equally for the needs of the Gentiles, as He does the descendants of Abraham?" They were reminded that the Great Commission tasked them to preach the gospel to "every nation." According to Scripture, any believer who aspires to serve Jesus must give people of every race equal access to the Good News. This demonstrates true awareness. Similarly, you must show equal concern to the different kinds of people in your sphere—your school, workplace, and community.

Several years ago I was part of the teaching faculty of a large pastors' conference. One of the other guest speakers had great content, but his delivery was lacking. Although the conference had roughly fifty percent men and fifty percent women, he kept saying "men of God" throughout his sermons. This pastor never acknowledged the women in the room. The phrase "men of God" was used to challenge and encourage the men that they belonged to God and must represent God in their ministry. The fact that he never gave equal or reasonable acknowledgment of the women by using the similar phrase "women of God" or any closely related term created a major annoyance with the attendees. The conference host was so put out he couldn't control his displeasure.

The erring speaker spoke the first night and the next morning before quickly flying out to his next ministry appointment. The conference host had no opportunity to speak with him, so he shared his frustration with me. I'll never forget the pain on his face when he said, "Doesn't God care about His daughters? Aren't our wives, sisters, and daughters equally important to God? Aren't they working alongside of us in the trenches of ministry? Why couldn't that pastor recognize their presence here and their value to God and to us?"

His rhetorical questions were all on point. And while he was noticeably troubled, his concern came from a healthy place. This just goes to show you that when you don't show awareness for the

people in your midst it hurts them. When people are not recognized, especially in a ministry setting, some folks will internalize
their feelings in a way that questions God's love for them. Those
questions point to hurt. In the case of my friend's conference, the
women felt as if they weren't even in the room. They felt unimportant to the speaker. The speaker had no idea he was creating such
pain. I heard him speak before this conference. He did the same
thing in that setting. The room was equally filled with men and
women, but he only recognized the men, using the same term,
"men of God." He had a huge blind spot in this area and a healthy
confrontation would have been helpful to his personal growth.
Awareness is a powerful tool toward building a cross-cultural life.

Self-awareness is the ability to hold a mirror in front of you so
you can form an accurate interpretation of what's truly there. The
mirror can come in the form of people. Have you ever asked your
friends, coworkers, or family members to critique your interaction
with people of other races? We are unable to see our backs, so we
have to rely on others to tell us if the backs of our shirts are wrin-
kled or stained. A friend can easily provide you with a few pointers
to help you grow in your cross-cultural awareness. This assumes
your friend or coworker is cross-cultural.

If there's no one in your life who can hold up a mirror for you,
piercing questions can also be used. For example, do you initiate
conversations with people of other races? Have you ever had dinner
guests of another race at your home more than once? How about
this one: How often do people of another race compliment you?

These questions are meant to help you identify your place on
the journey of self-awareness. If the answers are disappointing, rest
assured you can change. The fact the Great Commission calls you

to share the gospel across cultural and ethnic lines is an indication that diversity is in your DNA. To positively respond to the call to value diversity, which all Christians have received on a cellular level, you must yield to the Holy Spirit's process of change. The process requires taking a hard look at yourself and the way you relate to people of other cultures. You must either change or face cross-cultural irrelevance and extinction.

It's good to know diversity can be learned and you can change. Reinhold Niebuhr, H. Richard Niebuhr's brother, taught us the serenity prayer for circumstances like this: "God, give us grace to accept with serenity the things that cannot be changed, courage to change the things which should be changed, and the wisdom to distinguish the one from the other."[3] Your views toward others, their value, and your need to have an awareness of your responsibility to build a social relationship with them are not impossible feats. Your previous lack of cross-cultural skills can be changed and you don't need to blame anyone for your previously limited perspective. English author and satirist Douglas Noel Adams once said, "When you blame others, you give up your power to change." Because the Holy Spirit is with you, comforting, guiding, and assisting, you can change.

The Antioch Church became a multicultural expression of the Body of Christ because a number of the believers showed courage in crossing cultures. Although that was not the norm in the Jerusalem Church, their awareness of the need for all people to hear and experience the gospel drove them across cultural barriers. These believers changed because they saw the need and welcomed the opportunity to connect across cultural lines. If they can change you can change. Luke, the author of the Book of Acts, tells us, "The

Lord's hand was with them, and a great number of people believed and turned to the Lord" (Acts 11:21). In other words, the ability to achieve a cross-cultural expression of God's love is evidence of God's grace at work through people (Acts 11:23).

Take Ownership

As Christians we've been commissioned to live and breathe diversity wherever we find ourselves. If you believe the Great Commission reflects the longing of Jesus' heart for a diverse family, you must take complete ownership of it. This command is for you. Diversity must become one of *your* personal lifestyle goals. My friend Fred was sincerely committed to the goal of distributing all his gospel coins. He achieved it through hard work and a laser-like focus. Though building cross-cultural friendships does take hard work and a laser-like focus, the level of difficulty depends on your present level of cross-cultural experience and your eagerness to take ownership of God's call to live a multicultural life.

A multicultural life is the exact opposite of individualism. Our sinful nature calls us to worship self and seek the promotion of self-supremacy. That's individualism. The gospel calls us to live our lives in combat against individualism. This is done by embracing community. Community is a place of belonging. It's a place of acceptance and fellowship with others. It's a place where we can be real with one another without fear of rejection. Instead of us forming multicultural communities once we gravitate away from individualism, we've allowed the magnetic pull of monocultural communities to draw us in. Although living in community is better than individualism, living in monocultural communities is not the preferred model of Jesus.

The reason churches are largely monocultural is because it takes less work for those of the same culture to come together in a social setting. It takes no thought to form a segregated community. No real effort is required, but it's not acceptable. The Bible emphatically declares it's not. We're called to demonstrate the unity for which Christ died on the cross. Remember, "for God so loved the *world* that He gave His only Son." That's why Paul declared, "There is neither Jew nor Greek, slave nor free, male nor female, for you are all one in Christ Jesus" (Galatians 3:28). This verse clearly illustrates that we must strive to make diversity a reality in our everyday lives.

Though work is required to build a multicultural life, we cannot lose sight of our calling to do this. From Genesis to Revelation, God has made His intention very clear. The Scripture opens with God's intention to bless *all peoples on Earth* through Abraham (Genesis 12:3), and it closes with His desire for the healing of the nations (Revelation 22:2). God cannot make it any clearer than this. Our Father wants a diverse family.

As servants of God we must practice acceptance by taking ownership of God's will, desire, and intentions in matters of race relations. To do this, we can ask ourselves two questions: Why are we together? And, how are we to be together?

Why Are We Together?

The members of the new church planted at Antioch must have asked themselves this question: Why are we together? They had no prototype. No other churches, mosques, or synagogues were modeling diversity. It was unusual to see people who were racially, culturally, and ethnically different from one another worshipping the same God, at the same time, and under the same roof. This question gives everyone a theological and philosophical reason for choosing to be together, and it's the same reason the Jewish believers shared their faith with the Gentiles in the first place (Acts 11:20). The Jewish believers wanted the Gentiles to know and serve this Jesus who they came to know as Savior. Jesus was *the* answer as to why they were together.

If honoring and serving Jesus became the focus of the Church at Antioch, there would be no need to have a Hebraic Christian center at one end of the city and a Gentile Christian center at the other end. Since language was not a barrier among the congregation, there was no reason for race and culture to become barriers. This church became a prototype. It embodied the command to "Love your neighbor as yourself." This would be a witness to the Roman Empire and beyond that Jesus could bring different kinds of people together. The choice to be together positioned the Antioch Church to become a witness of Christianity's ability to achieve racial and cultural harmony. The church must provide the same witness today, but it requires each of us to personally commit to the same ideal of building a cross-cultural community. Honoring Jesus must be the primary reason we want to get together and stay together.

I recently attended a formal banquet hosted by a Christian organization whose mission is to develop strong families. Before the dinner everyone walked around, mingling, greeting one another, and striking up impromptu conversations. I met a gentleman who I'll call

Henry. I'm not sure how the topic of our mutual families entered the conversation, but in a few minutes Henry whipped out a bunch of photos from his wallet proudly displaying his family. He was a husband, father, and grandfather. I was surprised to see his family looked like a general session of the United Nations. Though married for thirty-two years, Henry and his wife didn't have any biological children. They decided to adopt after the first few years of marriage. Their children represent the globe—white, Asian, black, and Hispanic.

Henry and his wife were white. I couldn't help myself, so I asked him a rather personal question: "Why did you and your wife adopt children of different races?" His answer was rather unusual. Henry told me his own parents were very prejudiced. They hated everyone who was different from them. After he and his wife got married and learned they couldn't have children, they decided to adopt kids from different parts of the world. "I decided that if the world was going to change people like my parents, it would start with us," Henry said. "We took on the fight against bigotry by becoming cross-cultural even when it wasn't fashionable some thirty years ago." This Christian man took a personal stance in answering the question: Why are we together? His answer was seen through his lifestyle choice of modeling who Jesus is to the world by the way he showed love to his diverse band of adopted children.

How Are We to Be Together?

At the heels of the first question, the second is posed. "How are we to be together?" If Jesus is the answer to the question why we are together, allowing His teachings to guide, shape, and equip the community must prove to be the answer to *how are we to be together.* In forming true multicultural communities there are two main building blocks we cannot ignore: authenticity and acceptance.

1. Authenticity

Authenticity speaks of realness, sincerity, and genuineness. There is no phony, hypocritical, or pretentious behavior when you're authentic with people. Hypocrisy is the opposite. A hypocrite is someone who pretends to have feelings, values, or beliefs they don't have. In Bible days, the word *hypocrite* was used to describe an actor on the stage. These actors spoke their lines from behind a mask. The audience and the ones to whom they were speaking never knew the real person. They knew what they said, but did not know who they really were. They were hidden behind a mask. A lack of authenticity makes us hypocrites. Never let that be said of you. Being branded a hypocrite is a pretty bad label. Strive to practice authenticity, especially across cultural lines. Let people see the sincerity and genuineness of your heart toward them and they'll take to you and a new friendship will quickly form.

The first time our church learned a worship song in Spanish was some twenty years ago. One of the young men in the congregation was of Puerto Rican descent. He fell in love with a young lady who began attending our church who was also Puerto Rican. Back then we did not have our own facilities. We rented space from a catering hall. Every Sunday morning we'd have to set up chairs, a PA system, children's church materials, and a myriad of other things well before worship began. We were a portable church with roughly five hundred members. Juan and Vicky approached me one day after worship with a request. To save money on having to rent a separate reception hall for their wedding, they asked if they could get married following a Sunday worship service in the same hall the church used. I said, "Absolutely, if the managers of the facility don't mind." Sure enough, they said yes and Juan and Vicky went into wedding-planning mode.

I was to be the officiating minister. I was quite excited, partly because I was the one who led them both to the Lord, independent of one another. About a month before the wedding Juan told me both of their grandparents and extended family would be coming to the worship service and then would stay afterward for the wedding. He shared that some of the older family members only spoke Spanish. He didn't make any special requests of us. It was just an FYI.

In preparation for the big day, I asked our worship team to learn and sing a few of the songs in Spanish to create a bilingual experience during worship. During the worship time that day my eyes came across one of the Spanish-speaking grandmothers as a worship song was being sung in her language. I saw tears rolling down her cheeks. The memory is still etched in my mind because I knew what her tears meant. It meant we were being authentic in our desire to create a place where she was welcomed. It also meant we wanted her to have a genuine encounter with God. That day I learned the value of authenticity as it relates to diversity.

2. Acceptance

Sociologists have proven that whenever physical separation among races exists, it further divides the races, making multiculturalism a harder feat to accomplish.[4] This reality is even more pronounced when separation occurs in a religious setting. This fact is what caused Dr. Martin Luther King Jr., to say, "We must face the sad fact that at eleven o'clock on Sunday morning when we stand to sing 'In Christ there is no East or West,' we stand in the most segregated hour of America."[5]

Although we have made major strides since Dr. King's observation on December 18, 1963, we still have a long way to go. Some studies indicate 14 percent of churches in America are considered multiracial, with at least 20 percent of members coming from racial groups different from the congregation's majority race.[6] But this is just a drop in the bucket. With approximately 500,000 churches in the United States, using the 14 percent diversity number, that translates to 70,000 racially diverse churches. That seems like a lot. But when you subtract it from what remains, you are stunned to find out that 430,000 monoracial churches remain. We have much work to do as the Body of Christ.

Although we're not living in a segregated America, we are living in a religiously separated America. Our separation is by choice. Separation reinforces suspicion, myths, and all kinds of legends. Separation distances us from one another socially, opening us to misgivings and other false notions. Separation sends the signal, "You don't belong here. You're not welcome. You're not wanted. This is not your church." On a deeper level it communicates preference. The outsider hears this unspoken message loud and clear: "I prefer to not worship with you. I prefer for you to not worship with me." No matter how you interpret the message, separation across racial and cultural lines communicates rejection on a deeper level.

The flip side is quite powerful though. Acceptance of someone in worship across racial and cultural lines is a big deal. Acceptance is seen as friendliness. You view the person of another race as your social peer, without a paternalistic mindset or seeing him or her as a mission project. The accepted person feels a sense of belonging and community. Acceptance sends the signal you feel comfortable around that person, especially in a social setting.

Acceptance and belonging are significant building blocks to a multicultural community. People must be made to feel they belong. Social awkwardness is very uncomfortable. You feel like an outsider, a misfit, or a member of another community. You feel like you don't belong. In those instances, it will take hard work and will require you to take risks of being rejected in order to make some headway in building community. But if an insider takes you under his or her wing, by personally accepting and mentoring you in how to fit into his or her group, it becomes easier.

When a local Presbyterian church placed Pastor Stephanie (a pseudonym), a white American woman who recently graduated seminary, into a predominantly Chinese congregation, the cultural sparks began to fly. The congregation felt misunderstood and she felt rejected. The cultural divide quickly widened as the church resisted all the new pastor's attempts to improve its ministry. The congregation felt their pastor lacked the ability to minister to them because she wasn't Chinese and knew nothing about their culture. In danger of failing at her first ministry assignment, Pastor Stephanie needed to act swiftly. To avoid further cultural alienation, she humbly asked one of the leading families in the church to mentor her on Chinese culture. Her hope was to become more culturally adept and even learn some Bible verses in Mandarin.

Huang Fu and his wife opened their home to Pastor Stephanie. As he recounted the story to me, he shared how he and the pastor met weekly for tea and lessons about Chinese culture. There were many comical moments stemming from her attempt to learn to speak some words in Mandarin, but these only served to endear her to the congregation. For example, one time she placed the guttural sounds in the wrong spot during her pronunciation as she tried to end a sermon in Mandarin. As Pastor Stephanie preached on the account of Jesus raising Lazarus from the dead, her mispronunciation and incorrect placement of emphasis in the words ended up with Jesus telling Lazarus, "Don't come out of the grave! Stay there!" The congregation roared with laughter. The sermon unintentionally became a huge success. God used the language blunder of a white American female pastor to knit her heart with that of a mostly Asian congregation. That day she was accepted into their community.

If you are taking risks to develop cross-race friendships, be patient. God is at work in all our hearts. Who knows? It may take a blunder like Pastor Stephanie's to open the heart of the group so you'll find acceptance.

The challenge on your part is not to fall prey to limiting yourself to monocultural relationships. If you do, your behavior will reflect this as a limitation in building community with others. You must act differently from the fallen world in which we live because you have been made a new creation in Christ Jesus. Show awareness, take ownership in the call to model diversity wherever you go, and slowly but surely you'll grow as an agent of racial reconciliation.

CHAPTER THREE

Defining Moments

A ndrew Young Jr. was an activist for the civil rights movement. He was one of the lieutenants and strategists for Dr.
Martin Luther King Jr. Young became a member of Congress, mayor of Atlanta, and U.S. ambassador to the United
Nations. Prior to holding these high-profile jobs, positions that
afforded him significant opportunities to connect across cultures
and nations, Young began his career as a pastor. In a July 2016
interview with Atlanta radio station WABE, Young reflected on
his amazing career and how he, an African American, born in the
racially oppressive South (New Orleans, Louisiana), achieved such
a broad impact across cultures and races. There was a defining
moment—a pivotal conversation—he had with his dad early in life.
Young recounted:

The Olympics have always been a major influence in my life. When I was 4 years old, the Nazi party…headquarters was fifty yards from where I was born. And my father was explaining to me why these people were "heiling" Hitler and singing "Deutschland Uber Alles." And they had on the brown shirts and their swastikas. And my father said, "Nazism is a form of white supremacy, and white supremacy is a sickness. And you don't get upset or worry about sick people. Don't let them get you angry or upset, because then you can catch the sickness." He explained it to me in such a way that I've forever been grateful.

This was '36, 1936, and I was four years old. So he took me to see the Movietone News version of the Olympics. And Jesse Owens won the first race. And Hitler was to have given him the medal, and instead Hitler and all of his storm troopers left the stadium. And my father said, "But you see: Jesse Owens didn't let that get him upset; he just went on and won three more gold medals." (Laughs) It was one of the earliest moments in life I remember.[1]

Young's conversation with his dad made it clear: he had to make a choice. Would he become a person who hates or a person who loves people? Thankfully, he made the decision to become a man who loves people—all kinds of people. This decision became the launching pad from which his remarkable career took off.

Defining moments are pivotal times in which a life-altering decision is made. You cannot predict when these moments happen.

They just do. Conversations or experiences are usually what trigger them. One thing is certain, after these moments occur, you will never be the same again. They are so real and transformational they literally set a new trajectory for your life.

Defining Moments Redefine Life

A few years back I was invited to teach a leadership seminar to a group of medical missionaries. These doctors were stationed in some forty countries all over the world. They chose to gather in the Dominican Republic since it was one of their main hubs. Over lunch, one of the missionaries from Columbia shared a most unusual story with me about a couple in his church. The husband had an affair after three years of marriage. Knowing he was wrong, he quickly broke off the relationship with the other woman. Out of guilt and conviction, he made a full confession to his wife. She was extremely angry and distraught, and rightly so. After a few weeks of wrestling with her disappointment and anger, she forgave him. Before she forgave him, however, she put on her wedding dress, walked into her backyard, and in the quietness of the morning, she made a vow. She said, "Jesus, I know you hate divorce. I will forgive my husband and remain with him. But from now on, you are my husband. He is not!"

Afterward, she came inside the house and announced to her husband she had forgiven him. He was delighted, though he was still angry at himself for violating his marriage covenant and causing his wife so much pain. As time went on, the husband realized there was no warmth, intimacy, or affection from his wife. They went from counselor to counselor in search of help. Finally, they came to this missionary, who was their youth pastor years earlier. Knowing their story of bouncing from one counselor to another, he said, "Let me fast for three days, and then I'll meet with you guys. Please don't tell me anything now. Wait until we meet again." They parted company.

During those three days, the Lord spoke to him about their situation. God gave the missionary a vision of the wife donning a wedding dress and making a vow that Jesus was her husband and not the man she married. When they reconnected he shared this remarkable experience with them. She affirmed the accuracy of his vision. He then told her when she made that vow she was altering the Scriptures and by doing so, her misguided pledge redefined her life and the course of her marriage. He validated the biblical metaphor of Jesus being a groom and the church being His bride as true, but not in the sense she meant it.

The Apostle John said, "I saw the Holy City, the new Jerusalem, coming down out of heaven from God, prepared as a bride beautifully dressed for her husband. And I heard a loud voice from the throne saying, 'Look! God's dwelling place is now among the people, and he will dwell with them'" (Revelation 21:2–3). The whole Church is Jesus' bride, not one person. Words have life. Jesus taught us they create realities, new realities—good or bad (Matthew 15:18).

When this hurting wife made that vow in her backyard, it was a defining moment. Her marriage took another downward turn. Fortunately, the missionary knew how to handle his vision. It was to be another defining moment that would redefine their marriage and life. He led the wife in another vow. This time, the vow was to align itself with the Scriptures. The wife rescinded the earlier vow and made a new vow to be a loving, caring, and affectionate wife to her husband. Likewise, the husband renewed his vow to be a faithful, loving husband to his wife. The marriage turned around and began to blossom.

One of my takeaways from this story is that neither the wife nor the husband knew the silent, implicit messages she was sending due to her earlier vow. This is often the case with our negative feelings toward members of certain races. Our views, formed in the past, often out of pain, myth, biases, or just plain old prejudice, affect how we perceive people today. And often we are unaware of it.

In his book *Blink* Malcolm Gladwell says: "Over the past few years, a number of psychologists have begun to look more closely at the role these kinds of unconscious—or, as they like to call them, implicit—associations play in our beliefs and behavior, and much of their work has focused on a very fascinating tool called the Implicit Association Test (IAT)."[2] The IAT is based on the observation "we make connections much more quickly between pairs of ideas that are already related in our minds than we do between pairs of ideas that are unfamiliar to us."[3] The Race IAT measures your unconscious attitude toward race, which may be different than your conscious attitude.

I appreciate instruments like this. However, we Christians have the Holy Spirit living on the inside. This means we have a built-in IAT. The Holy Spirit convicts us of sin and prompts us to abide by the Scriptures in the way we treat others. We just have to be sensitive to Him and remain vigilant in our approach to live up to the standard of Sacred Scripture.

Align Yourself with Scripture

Defining moments have the innate ability to redefine life. Perhaps you have hit an impasse in your ability to love across cultural lines. Take a moment and reflect on your life. Was there a time you had a painful cross-cultural experience—one you've never gotten over? Don't overlook the venom that can run through your life when prejudice strikes. You may have unconsciously thought hate or separation from people of that race was a good anti-venom. Looking back, you now realize it was not. You can take control of your life right now. Don't let painful memories drive you into a monocultural life.

Khadijah, an African American woman, was part of a high school gospel choir at the local Catholic school. To her surprise, one day her vigorous clapping to the rhythmic music landed her in the principal's office. She was told, "We don't clap like that in Catholic school." Khadijah left the office thinking, "You feel something negative about my culture and now you're imposing it on me." She admitted to me, "Pastor, I started a ten-year journey and conscious sense of prejudice—prejudice against me. I no longer viewed myself first as a woman. I now saw myself as others saw me: black was first and a woman was second. Although I was able to formulate some cross-cultural relationships, I was always guarded and on the defense for any possible racial slurs or cultural jabs." Khadijah's painful experience was a defining moment for her—a negative one.

As life would have it, she found herself sitting at Christ Church one Sunday morning. God would not let her off the hook. Through the ministry of the Word, she had to face her disobedience head-on. She could not set cultural or racial limits to her love. Thankfully, Khadijah redefined her life by making a new vow. Her love was no longer going to be discriminating. She was going to love people across cultures, the way Jesus wanted her to. Looking back, she realized that particular Sunday was a defining moment. She made a commitment to live her life according to the Bible and not based on her pain.

Making New Confessions

Words are powerful when spoken in faith. That is what confessions are. You can change your life by making a new confession. Zacchaeus, a known sinner who lived outside the parameters of a godly life, did it. Jesus was passing through Jericho one day. A huge crowd gathered preventing Zacchaeus, a short man, from seeing Jesus. Being resourceful, he ran ahead and climbed a sycamore-fig tree to see him. The moment Jesus got to the spot where Zacchaeus was, He looked up and said, "Zacchaeus, come down immediately. I must stay at your house today" (Luke 19:5). Surprised at the fact Jesus was going to dine at the home of Zacchaeus, this known scoundrel, all the people started murmuring against the judgment of Jesus. It was severely flawed, they thought.

What the crowd didn't know was by the time Zacchaeus shimmied down the tree he had experienced a defining moment. He had become born again. His reality and worldview changed. Jesus was now his Lord and Savior. Knowing and hearing the crowd's disapproval of him, in light of Jesus' invitation to dine at his home, Zacchaeus said, "Look, Lord! *Here and now* I give half of my possessions to the poor, and if I have cheated anybody out of anything, I will pay back four times the amount" (Luke 19:8, italics mine). Zacchaeus was a changed man. There would be no delay in aligning his life and actions with the Scriptures. Exodus 22:1 teaches us a penitent thief must restore the stolen property by fourfold. There would be no negotiating or attempt to reason away his bad actions. Zacchaeus meant business. He was changed.

Don't Delay Changing!

Have you been changed? Are you really serious about following Jesus all the way? Even across cultures and races? Defining moments challenge us to put away our excuses and take up our cross, regardless of who wronged us or who we wronged. We must grow, and growth demands change. Like Zacchaeus, Khadijah's change was immediate.

At the 2001 World Conference Against Racism, several leaders called for the public apology of Western powers for four hundred years of slavery. On the second day of this eight-day conference, Nigerian president Olusegun Obasanjo addressed the challenge by saying, "We must demonstrate the political will and assume the responsibility for the historical wrongs that are owed to the victims of slavery, that an apology be extended by states which actively practiced and benefited themselves from slavery."[4]

History tells us Nigeria was a former British colony. Joschka Fischer, formerly Germany's foreign minister, made an admission of historic wrongs because he saw how it would help restore victims and their descendants "the dignity of which they were robbed." He then went on to say, "I should therefore like to do that here and now on behalf of the Federal Republic of Germany."[5] That was a defining moment for Germany, Nigeria, and other world leaders. This moment announced a shift in perspective—the adoption of a new paradigm—one that would be brighter, fuller, and improved.

The greatest defining moment is when you accept Christ as your Savior. Your life is forever changed. You have become a new creation, a distinctly different person—a new person. The old person is gone and a new one has emerged (2 Corinthians 5:17).

Back in the late 1960s the Red Cross was gathering supplies, medicine, clothing, and food for the suffering people of Biafra (now an eastern state of Nigeria). Inside one of the boxes that showed up at a collection center one day was a letter. It said, "We have recently been converted and because of our conversion we want to try to help. We won't ever need these again. Can you use them for something?" Inside the box were several Ku Klux Klan sheets. The Red Cross cut them into strips and eventually used them to bandage the wounds of black victims in Africa. There is no doubt about it. That was a defining moment for the former KKK guy and later, the Red Cross worker.

Defining Moments Must Start Somewhere

In January 2015, there was a vicious terrorist attack in France. Three terrorists killed seventeen innocent people and injured another twenty-two people. The police killed the three assailants the same day. A few months later, France moved from one painful state to another. Paris was turned on its emotional head when it was hit with three suicide bombers and several mass shootings within minutes of each other. When it was all over, approximately 130 people were killed and 368 people were wounded. The city was in mourning. The Parisians felt anger, uncertainty, fear, distrust of others, and other painful emotions directed toward Muslims because of what these radicalized extremists did.

One week after the attack, an unidentified Muslim man stood blindfolded in the center of Paris. Next to him was a sign that read, "I'm Muslim, but I'm told that I'm a terrorist. I trust you, do you trust me? If yes, hug me." CNN reported hundreds came up to him and hugged him. From the old to the young, both men and women hugged the man. Some people wept uncontrollably. They were searching for hope. They were searching for a moment where they could release their hatred toward Muslims or anyone whose beliefs and culture seemed unknown or unfamiliar to their way of life. The blindfolded stranger provided a defining moment for many Parisians to live again, which was the opposite of the suffocating pain brought on by hate.

This blindfolded man's actions offered the French people a way of escape. When interviewed, the unidentified man said, "I deeply feel for all the victims' families. I want to tell you that [being] 'Muslim' doesn't necessarily mean 'terrorist.' A terrorist is a terrorist, someone willing to kill another human being over nothing. A Muslim would never do that. Our religion forbids it."[6]

The video of this blindfolded man standing at the gathering place in Paris where mourners pay homage and tribute—the Place de la République—has been watched more than ten million times on Facebook and received 150,000 likes in two days. His bold actions became a defining moment for many. Just imagine, if the actions of one Muslim man can garner this kind of response, what would happen if the whole Christian church suddenly attacked prejudice head-on by choosing to love people selflessly? Our positive actions would assure people—Christians and non-Christians alike—of the fact they can learn to love again.

Start with Repentance

There's never a good time to repent. We just have to do it when we realize we have been approaching people or life in the wrong way. Repentance follows conviction. The word *convict* means "to convince someone of the truth; to reprove; to accuse, refute, or cross-examine a witness." The Holy Spirit acts as a prosecuting attorney who exposes sin, reproves our unacceptable ways, convinces us we need a Savior, and we need to walk in the ways pleasing to our Savior. Conviction allows us to clearly sense the disparity between God's moral standards and how we've been living. The great English preacher Charles H. Spurgeon once said, "When we deal seriously with our sin, God will deal gently with us. When we hate what the Lord hates, he will soon make an end of it, to our joy and peace."[7]

God hates prejudice and monocultural living. To align with His view, which espouses diversity, we must repent, if we've been misaligned. Repentance is a change of our minds—a reversal of thought. Repentance captures the principle of voluntary obedience to God. We now share His mind on things—everything. We can reset our lives. Repentance is the reset button. Press it.

Don't allow yourself to become hardened in your pain, by the fact you've been wronged, or even by the thought you can't forgive yourself for your past infractions. Author and pastor David Wilkerson said, "Likewise today, some Christians are content to merely exist until they die. They don't want to risk anything, to believe God, to grow or mature. They refuse to believe his Word, and have become hardened in their unbelief. Now they're living just to die."[8] Don't let this be you. Exercise repentance. Don't delay. Do it now!

John Chrysostom said, "Repentance is a medicine which destroys sin, a gift bestowed from heaven, an admirable virtue, a grace exceeding the power of laws."[9] When we repent, it is as if we can predict our own defining moment. No wonder Oswald Chambers wrote in his book *My Utmost for His Highest*, "the bedrock of Christianity is repentance. Strictly speaking, a man cannot repent when he chooses; repentance is a gift of God. The old Puritans used to pray for 'the gift of tears.' If ever you cease to know the virtue of repentance, you are in darkness. Examine yourself and see if you have forgotten how to be sorry."[10]

I would have loved to see Peter's face when Paul confronted him about his divisive behavior at the Antioch Church (Galatians 2:14). Peter's discomfort and cultural ignorance created a rift in the multiethnic congregation. Being the lead pastor, Paul wouldn't stand for it. The confrontation was public because the infraction was public. Peter was faced with a defining moment. Which path would he take? If he defended his prejudicial actions, he would be guilty of violating the Scriptures and also of harming the Body of Christ. He had to take the other path—the path of repentance leading to his personal development as an authentic reconciler. Although the letter to the Galatians does not spell out Peter's response, we can do a little forensic work to discover his reaction.

In Peter's first letter he writes, "Live as free men, but do not use your freedom as a cover-up for evil; live as servants of God. Show proper respect to everyone: Love the brotherhood of believers, fear God, honor the king" (Galatians 2:16–17). Bull's-eye! Peter hit the nail right on the head. Apparently he experienced a defining moment. His views toward diversity changed. Paul's confrontation played a part in tilting him toward a multicultural lifestyle. There were other contributing factors, but we cannot discount Paul's input. Peter's lifestyle and worldview became aligned with God's. Peter was not above repentance and repentance will prove just as potent in your life as it was in Peter's.

Repentance Is an Act of Humility

It takes humility to repent, but you'll be the better for it. Consider how things must have fared for Barnabas at his home church—the church at Antioch—after Paul's public confrontation of Peter. Peter's divisive behavior of eating solely with Jews and not Gentiles even influenced Barnabas. Paul wrote, "The other Jews joined him [Peter] in his hypocrisy, so that by their hypocrisy even Barnabas was led astray" (Galatians 2:13). I'm sure Barnabas had to repent too. There is no way he could have simply swept things under the rug, as a pastor at Antioch. He had to square things with the congregation.

Repentance must be seen as a positive act and not a negative one. Repentance is a change of view. It's not simply mourning over the past; it is a joyful looking to the future. Here too, the Scriptures are silent regarding Barnabas' repentance or his actions to reconnect with the congregation. Being a pastor, I understand your ability to influence your congregation rests on the trust factor. If they trust you, you can influence them. Conversely, if they don't trust you, you may be the finest teacher in the world, but there will be a huge emotional disconnect between you and the flock. To bridge the gap repentance is mandatory.

Your repentance will help rebuild the bonds of trust. It will also remind the people that anyone can make mistakes, even leaders. It will teach others how easy it is to live behind our cultural walls and think we're pleasing the Lord. But repentance is an invitation into God's country—the place where equal status and value of people is modeled by how we live. Any action of repentance on Barnabas' part would only have buoyed the value of multicultural ministry. It is easy to see his renewed perspective was underscored by his changed behavior regarding the ministry style needed to build a thriving multiethnic church.

Don't be afraid to repent if you need to. Repentance is a game-changer. It's a gift from God to you. Use it and you'll find yourself experiencing a defining moment.

CHAPTER FOUR

Rebuilding the Bridge

Pain is unpredictable. It makes you do things you could never anticipate. When the pain stems from victimization, especially the kind that can accurately be labeled as race related, it is extremely difficult to get that wounded person to become cross-cultural. That person wears pain as a medal, a badge of courage, almost proudly displaying the reason for living a mono-cultural lifestyle.

I remember once I was in the middle of a sermon series on diversity and I was at an impasse. I had to find a way to help people rebuild the bridge that would lead them across the cultural and racial divide into a multicultural life. So, I spent quite a bit of time praying and fasting, seeking God's wisdom regarding how to help victims of prejudice break free from the pain it caused them.

After a couple of days, an idea came to me as I was reading about Jesus washing His disciples' feet (see John 13). As the story goes, Jesus got up from the evening meal, wrapped a towel around His waist, washed His disciples' feet, and then dried them with the towel. Peter, the infamously outspoken disciple, objected by telling Jesus, "No, you shall never wash my feet" (verse 8). For Peter, the idea of Jesus washing his feet was inconceivable. First, foot washing was a menial task performed by servants. In fact, the renowned New Testament Greek scholar Leon Morris points out "[foot washing] was so menial a Hebrew slave was not required to perform it, though a Gentile slave might be."[1] Second, Jesus was *his* Master, not the other way around. Jesus responded to Peter's objection, saying, "Unless I wash you, you have no part with me," so Peter gave in.

Jesus was teaching the disciples a tremendous lesson: serving someone else is a powerful display of love. Hearts become vulnerable during a foot-washing ceremony. The Scripture says, "The evening meal was being served, and the devil had already prompted Judas Iscariot, son of Simon, to betray Jesus" (John 13:2). Jesus gave Judas one last opportunity to come clean and get free from his scheme to give Him up for thirty pieces of silver. He said, "A person who has had a bath needs only to wash his feet; his whole body is clean. And you are clean, though not every one of you" (verses 10-11). Cold-blooded Judas managed to keep a dirty heart while having clean feet. He could not find room within his soul to ask for forgiveness for the sin of disloyalty and betrayal. Even though Judas did not respond to Jesus' foot washing with tears of repentance and confession, Jesus' act was still an undeniable symbol of humility and readiness to forgive, especially from a status of social superiority.

After reading the story again, I was sold. The act of foot washing is still a potent spiritual exercise that can produce a clean heart. Regardless of whether a person is the victimizer or the victim of a prejudicial act, foot washing can be a therapeutic practice if the Holy Spirit is involved. I decided to have two men—one white, the other black—wash each other's feet publicly to demonstrate forgiveness of the historic racial problems stemming from their forefathers.

I wanted the foot washing to set the stage for the congregation to open their hearts to Almighty God, who knew how to clean sin-stained hearts of racism. The act had to be presented as more than a historical occasion with Jesus and His disciples; it had to be positioned as a medicinal act that would unite with our faith to bring us to a place of freedom.

That Sunday morning, I was prepared with basin, towel, and a pitcher of water. Scott, an African American man, agreed to participate in this important teaching moment. I knew he struggled with cross-race friendships because of the destructive role racism played in his own family, so I asked him to share his story during the actual foot washing. His counterpart that morning was Ron, a white brother, who grew up with strong prejudice toward blacks. Only when he came to know Jesus as his Savior was his heart softened and accepting of blacks.

I instructed both men privately, "Guys, the goal of my sermon is to create a moment for hearts to be opened to accepting people of different races. This change of heart can come only when forgiveness is extended and received." I shared that forgiveness must be extended with honesty and full ownership of the wrongdoing in order for its healing power to be released. Similarly, I said forgiveness must be embraced so its curative effects can take root in the heart of the wounded person.

Then I laid out my plan to the two men: "I will explain to the congregation what foot washing means and then give each of you an opportunity to speak directly to the other as the representative for your race. For example, as Ron is seated facing you, Scott, and as you wash his feet, share with him how the prejudice from the white race has impacted you. But, when you finish, in your own words ask for his forgiveness for harboring ill will and anger toward him and members of his race."

We discussed how after Scott washed and dried Ron's feet the two would change places and go through the process again. This time Ron would wash Scott's feet while sharing his struggles and his need for forgiveness. Once the plan was clear, we walked into the sanctuary armed with a God-given illustration carrying the potential to free a lot of people from the baggage of prejudice.

As Scott washed Ron's feet, he choked up. He revealed that years of racial victimization led his father to abuse alcohol. He was mistreated by whites solely on the basis of his skin color. Scott spoke about his anger toward whites and his need to remove the barrier preventing him from connecting with whites in the way he knew God wanted him to. His tears fell into the basin, mixing with the water used to wash Ron's feet. Scott's heartfelt plea for forgiveness echoed throughout the sanctuary. Because Ron was acting as a representative of the white race, his forgiveness was critical for Scott's healing. Without hesitation, Ron forgave Scott. A palpable ripple effect swept across the sanctuary as other African Americans allowed their racially torn hearts to be washed by Ron's all-important words of forgiveness.

After we composed ourselves, the two men switched places. This time Scott sat in the chair and Ron wrapped the towel around his waist and held the pitcher of water in his hands. As he poured water over Scott's feet, I could sense Ron's heart was being emptied of all the prejudiced feelings of superiority toward other races. Ron shared his childhood experiences of growing up with ideas of white supremacy. He admitted he'd embraced that philosophy and behaved accordingly throughout his life. But on this day he said, "Can you forgive me for thinking, acting, and treating you as lesser than me? I realize I need your forgiveness to be the man I want to be. Will you free me today?"

This was a holy moment. Forgiveness and repentance were gifts wrapped and handed to us that morning. That Sunday morning, the entire congregation received the gift of tears as the power of forgiveness washed over our hearts. When the words "I forgive you" left Scott's lips, he freed Ron and every member of the white race who sat there in need of forgiveness from the enslavement of prejudice. At that moment, the Holy Spirit took over the service, and it was no longer under my pastoral leadership. He was now in full control and I was a silent observer. I watched. I wept. I, too, was healed.

Forgiveness Is a Gift from God!

Can you see forgiveness is a gift from God? Somehow the cancer of pain is surgically removed as we utter these simple yet life-changing words, "I forgive you." The words are not an admission of weakness, as some have falsely thought. Neither are the words an indication you've been duped into accepting an apology from some undeserving culprit. Forgiveness is a personal gift. It's a gift you can give to yourself anytime. You can even receive the benefits of forgiveness when no apologies have been uttered by the erring party. Forgiveness of this kind is acknowledging the brokenness of people and giving them an unrequested pardon based on that reality. You can become imprisoned by waiting for an apology. It may not come because the erring party is so immature, complicated, hardened in selfishness, or merely unaware of his infraction. This is when you must recognize forgiveness is a gift to you from God. And, if truth be told: forgiveness is also a gift to you from you.

A few years back a beautiful bouquet of flowers was delivered to one of our staff members. Melissa was a single woman in her early thirties. She'd never been married and she had no children. Everyone smiled and cheered for Melissa because the flowers symbolized that "love was in the air." Melissa had some guy in her life she'd hidden from us, or so we thought. A few of us asked, almost in unison, who's the lucky guy? Her response was unexpected. Melissa said, "I sent the flowers." Melissa called up a local florist and ordered the beautiful flowers herself for delivery at the office. Although it was a tad unusual we understood she wanted to feel special. Since there was no guy in her life at that moment she sent the flowers to herself. Melissa was thinking, "I don't need a guy to send me flowers to feel special. I can send myself flowers."

Forgiveness operates the same way. You don't need a special foot washing service or an event to get you into a mood to ask for forgiveness. Granted, those moments are special. But since forgiveness is a gift from God available twenty-four hours a day, seven days a week, you can access it anytime. Without it you'll stand immobile on one side of the multicultural bridge unwilling and unable to walk across or even step foot on it.

Jesus encouraged His audience along the path of diversity when He told the moving parable of The Good Samaritan (Luke 10:25-37). A man was brutally beaten, robbed, and left at the side of the road to die. The man was unnamed and unidentified regarding his race, ethnicity, or home town. Jesus wanted His hearers to draw a lesson from His story that would induce immediate and irreversible change. They had to learn their need to "love your neighbor as yourselves" (Luke 10:27).

As the story continued, the wounded traveler lay by the roadside and a priest came walking by, sighted him, and crossed to the other side of the road. Unmoved by the stranger's plight, the priest went on his way. A Levite (an assistant of sorts to a priest) traveling on the same road did the same thing as the priest. He spotted the wounded man, who was desperate for medical attention, and he crossed the road and kept on his way. He too was unmoved by human suffering, or at least that man's suffering. Lastly, a Samaritan came upon the dying stranger. He stopped, attended to the wounded man's medical needs, and then placed the stranger on his donkey. The Samaritan's mercy, love, and empathy didn't stop there; he took the man to an inn and paid for the man's stay and care. He told the innkeeper that upon his return from his business trip he would swing by and pay any overage that existed for the stranger. Jesus ended the story by asking: "Which of these three do you think was a neighbor to the man who fell into the hands of robbers?" (Luke 10:36)

The question was rhetorical. But there was a real zinger embedded in the story. Jesus' audience was largely Jewish. The longstanding resentment and anger between Jews and Samaritans was a well-known social problem. They couldn't stand each other. The fact that Jesus made the good guy in His story a Samaritan was really tightening the screws. The lesson presented by the parable was a call to love others, particularly those who are dissimilar from you—or even hated and despised by you. Jesus purposefully omitted the wounded man's race or other cultural identifiers. He threw down the gauntlet in front of His audience. He wanted them to build or rebuild the bridge of reconciliation.

Excuses Get Very Complicated!

I can just imagine Jesus' audience shifting from one foot to the other in their discomfort. Their minds were racing to come up with plausible excuses to justify their hardened hearts. They had made little to no movement across the cultural divide. What excuses could they give? At what point would they surrender to the thought: no more excuses? Jesus told this parable in response to an expert's question, "What must I do to inherit eternal life?" The questioner was an expert in the Law. This person is akin to our modern day attorney. He was well-versed at finding loopholes allowing him to escape the straightforward commands of God.

The whole controversy surrounding the "Black Lives Matter" movement can be best understood in light of the parable of the Good Samaritan. Blacks became infuriated with the devaluing of their lives, by the ease with which others committed racial crimes against them. Hence "Black Lives Matter" was formed to protest and bring attention to that reality. Justice is being sought and demanded. Admittedly, the phrase creates a lot of unanswered questions such as, "Don't all lives matter?" The answer is, absolutely. The police objected by saying, "Blue lives matter." Police officers have a hard job. There's no question about that. Every day they go to work they put their lives on the line. Will they return safely to their homes and families each night? That is a very difficult question to face every single day.

The social unrest between the Black Lives Matter Movement and police was exacerbated by pitting these phrases, and the people shouting them, against each other. If we all heeded the challenge of Jesus to love our neighbors as ourselves, there would be no need to say, "Black lives matter"; "Blue lives matter"; "All lives matter"; or even "Lives Matter." The facts and value of human life would speak for themselves. The stark reality exists; however, too many people across the racial divide are making a lot of excuses about why they cannot and will not love their neighbors as themselves. After a while these excuses become very complicated and get convoluted.

Pain is one of those complicated excuses—the pain of victimization that is. I'm not being unsympathetic about the travesty of racial injustices or of someone's pain. I'm simply pointing out that no matter how you rationalize it or try to use pain as a basis to keep you from crossing the multicultural bridge, your complicated excuse is still wrong.

To help my congregation understand how to form and maintain healthy cross-race relationships we created a series of professional videos under the heading, *The Skin I Live In*. Each three-minute video features a person giving a personal account about when he or she made the decision to forgive, or be forgiven, and then begin a multicultural lifestyle by walking across the multicultural bridge.

One of my favorite videos is the one featuring a Chinese brother, Alex.

Alex, now in his late sixties, tells the story of when his two daughters were growing up in New Jersey. Alex was born in China and grew up in a monoracial environment. When he migrated to America he hadn't fully embraced a multicultural life, even though he was a Christian and a preacher's kid. Diversity is not an issue in China, at least it wasn't back then. So, this need was not a real issue to him. At least not until God put His finger on it. In the video Alex recounts his angry outburst when he confronted his daughters one day about their playing with the non-Chinese kids in the neighborhood. He shouted, "Didn't I tell you not to play with those kids? Our neighbors have even brought it to my attention!" Apparently Alex's Chinese neighbors also held the same flawed perspective.

Tears streamed down Alex's face as he shared his daughters' response. They said, "Daddy, they are people too." Alex said his little girls were so brave to tell him that. They continued, "Didn't you say that Jesus said we ought to love our neighbors as ourselves. You're not doing that." More tears came. On the video, he then paused to regain composure. His excuses for maintaining a monocultural life were destroyed by two little girls. Alex began to slowly and steadily walk across the bridge of reconciliation. Today, he's a wonderful example of an authentic reconciler. It all started when he was challenged to face his prejudice head on.

Reconciliation Is Social and Public

The fact the Samaritan in the parable in Luke 10 attended to the wounded stranger, placing him on his donkey even while walking through the public square to register him at the inn, communicates that reconciliation is a social and public act. I mean, you cannot say you are a cross-cultural person if your social and public life says otherwise. The priest and Levite didn't stop. Why? Perhaps they each thought, "Why should I stop? This man is not one of my parishioners. I have no obligation toward him." Maybe they thought the man was mortally wounded and any contact with the dead would render them unclean based on Levitical grounds.

While we can't be quite sure about their reasoning, we do know for sure they wanted nothing to do with the wounded stranger. After all, too many questions would arise if they had been seen in public with this person. Jesus made a strong point. If you really love your neighbor as yourself, your love must go public at some point. It can't be a private, secretive position. That's not reconciliation. Reconciliation is not a veiled meeting no one is to know about. It is a public event. It is a social event. A business meeting with internationals or a racially blended group is not a display of "loving your neighbor as yourself." It will only mean that when you personally choose to connect with a person in a social setting where the occasion has little or nothing to do with furthering your business opportunities. Reconciliation will only be meaningful when your motive is strictly designed to deepen your cross-race relationship.

To a multicultural person being seen in a public space, away from the office, church, or school is a non-issue. You are after relationship and couldn't care less that someone from your family or racial group sees you fraternizing with a person outside your race or culture. Even if you're asked by a member of your race what you were doing eating at the diner with that person, you wouldn't shift from one foot to the other trying to come up with a plausible solution to justify being sighted in public with someone of another racial group. You'd defend your choice to meet socially without guilt or remorse.

The Need for Forgiveness

Anybody can hate. It's easy to hate. It hardly takes work to hate. Just like it's easier to destroy a bridge than build one. Old bridges are usually demolished with dynamite or large sections are skillfully removed by contractors in short order. The replacement bridge may take years to erect and millions of dollars to fund. If you're going to build or rebuild the reconciliation bridge after a major bout with prejudice you will have to forgive the offense.

Forgive means *to let go*; *to set free*; *to release*. The image reflects the opening of a door to a caged bird so it can fly free. When forgiveness happens you quickly discover you were the caged bird all along. Therefore, forgiveness is for *you* and not necessarily for the person being forgiven.

To access forgiveness you must separate the issues that often make it unattractive. Forgiveness *does not* mean reconciliation, which is when the offended person assumes a full reunion must follow. Not necessarily. For example, in the case of a physically abusive marriage, forgiveness does not mean a reunion with your abuser must follow. You can forgive and still terminate the relationship. My point is simply this: forgiveness and reconciliation are entirely different from one another.

Forgiveness *does not* mean justice has been served or the elimination of justice has now occurred. Just because you forgave someone does not mean you should no longer expect or pursue justice. If forgiveness is whitewashing a wrong, then it is itself a wrong. If my next-door neighbor stole my car because he was jealous of me, I'm required by the Bible to forgive him. I have no problem with forgiving him even though it may be hard. But, I'm still moving forward in pressing charges against him.

God is not asking you to discard justice when you invoke forgiveness. Justice and forgiveness are both important to God. One doesn't cancel out the other. They cannot. God is equally committed to both practices. God requires us to act justly (Psalm 106:3; Micah 6:8) and to be forgiving (Matthew 6:12; Colossians 3:13). We're called to obey both commands. I can forgive my neighbor just as easily if he's behind prison bars or walking around scot free. I don't have to give up justice to practice forgiveness. They are different from one another.

Forgiveness *does not* mean the elimination of healthy boundaries. Boundaries are the property lines of the soul. Boundaries identify that you are a separate person having a separate identity, behavior, attitudes, desires, and choices from other people. Boundaries answer the question: "Where do I end and where does someone else begin?" We're responsible for our own feelings and thoughts and not someone else's. If you think that forgiveness means you must ignore your personhood by ignoring your need for proper boundaries then you are sadly mistaken.

Exercising Forgiveness

Our culture struggles to understand the power and the host of benefits associated with forgiveness because it's often confused by other issues. Forgiveness is so important I had to spend some time explaining what it's not so you can fully appreciate what it is.

In Jesus' parable of the Good Samaritan, the man on the way to Jericho did not victimize himself. He was robbed and wounded by thieves. Similarly, in your painful experience with prejudice or intolerance you didn't wound yourself. Your emotional scars point to the fact that a person or a group mishandled you simply because you were different. I'm sorry it happened to you. Yet, as a Christ-follower you are well aware that Jesus said, "But if you do not forgive others their sins, your Father will not forgive your sins" (Matthew 6:15).

This is a pretty strong requirement you can't circumvent even though you've been hurt. Think about it for a minute. Given the nature of Jesus and His overwhelming love for you, there is absolutely no way He'd place an unreasonable burden on your shoulders. His requirement for you to forgive your abuser is for *your* good. Forgiveness is a pathway to a more rewarding life for you.

Forgiveness moves you toward wholeness and away from the painful past. Forgiveness helps you model authentic Christianity not only within your own culture, but across every culture. Learning to apply forgiveness can be complicated. But there are four steps you can take to make the forgiveness process clearer.

Part One: Hold the guilty party responsible.

Part Two: Recognize people are complicated.

Part Three: Surrender your right to get even.

Part Four: Change your attitude toward the guilty party.

1. Hold the guilty party responsible.

You can only forgive people when you hold them responsible. Forgiveness is made possible when you assign blame to the person, group, or race that wronged you. The way they handled you caused you injury. Recognize it. Admit it. If not you will remain immobile. You will not be able to build the multicultural bridge and cross into other cultures relationally. This chapter opened with the foot-washing story where Ron and Scott asked each other for forgiveness. To fully forgive one another, they had to acknowledge the past injustices brought on by people from the other race. Similarly, it's important you acknowledge you've been wronged. Don't sweep the injustice under the rug, ignoring the fact it occurred.

2. Recognize people are complicated.

We're all flawed, complicated, and broken in some way. We all have baggage. I joked with my congregation one Sunday saying, "We all have baggage. My baggage just looks nice because I've been walking with Jesus for thirty-five years. I have designer baggage, but it's still baggage just the same." Everyone laughed. The point was made.

Because of our brokenness we hurt others. The baggage is the compilation of the hurts, setbacks, and pain we carry with us. The moment you think you're above the possibility of causing pain in someone else's life, that is the moment you need to tell God "Move over so I can take a seat on the throne next to You." Moral crimes of hatred and prejudice occur because we're flawed people living in a broken culture. Recognizing that people, including you, are flawed helps you put the need to forgive others in perspective.

3. Surrender your right to get even.

The wronged party must surrender his or her right to get even. That's you. You can't fantasize about ways to hurt your abuser.

Running him down with your car won't help you. It would just grant you some quiet time behind bars. You'll have a prison ministry from the inside. You don't want that. This is why Paul wrote: "Do not take revenge, my dear friends, but leave room for God's wrath, for it is written: 'It is mine to avenge; I will repay,' says the Lord" (Romans 12:19).

Person to person forgiveness calls for you to abandon the right to revenge. That's God's responsibility. I've already tackled the false notion that forgiveness is the elimination of justice. This third ingredient in the formula of forgiveness has nothing to do with the topic of justice or its elimination. Surrendering the right to get even is simply saying: don't seek to take vengeance into your own hands by doing something equally wrong or hurtful as a form of payback. Don't practice street justice. Let God handle the matter in His own way.

4. Change your attitude toward the guilty party.

If you truly want to build a bridge across the rough waters of pain into a multicultural life, you must be willing to change your attitude toward the guilty party. Instead of hating the offender or his or her race, you begin to love and wish that person well.

In January 2015, nineteen-year-old Connor Hanifin of Toms River, New Jersey was sentenced to three and a half years in prison for the death of his best friend, Francis Duddy. Connor pleaded guilty to the vehicular homicide that caused the death of his friend who was a passenger in the car Connor was driving. He was driving drunk. Before the judge imposed the sentence in this emotional hearing, he allowed the victim's father, Dan Duddy Sr., to say something. He said, "You, Connor, have a responsibility to right yourself, as do we, and you can't do that, nor can we, without our forgiveness, it would be impossible…On behalf of all the people in my life, we give you a very high level of forgiveness, Connor."[2]

With his expression of forgiveness Dan Duddy Sr. completed the fourth and final part to releasing the power of forgiveness. The guilty party, Connor, with head down, voice soft from the mess his brokenness created, quietly read a statement to the court. It said, "Francis Duddy was my best friend. Though a shining piece of him will forever hold a place in our hearts, he is no longer with me because of what I did. I can only hope and pray other young people will learn from my mistake. I ask my family, the Duddy family and all of Francis' friends for forgiveness."[3] As the photographer captured a shot of Connor's face, a tear rolled down his cheek the moment he finished reading his statement. Forgiveness is not easy but it's necessary to move on to a brighter future. Although this example is not a race related one, the principle is still applicable.

The whole world witnessed the principle of forgiveness at work when Dylann Roof, a white supremacist, viciously gunned down nine African Americans in June 2015 while they were in prayer at the Emanuel AME church in Charleston, South Carolina. At the court hearing where Roof was being sentenced, Nadine Collier, whose seventy-year-old mother, Ethel Lance, was killed, was allowed to share her personal comments. Would her words widen the racial divide or rebuild a bridge weakened by this racist? The world anxiously watched and waited with expectation for her words to come.

Fueled by her strong Christian values, Nadine didn't spew out black empowerment rhetoric or hate-filled words decrying the ills of Roof's prejudiced worldview and actions. Instead she crossed the bridge into white, Hispanic, and Asian America by saying to Roof, "I forgive you." Her soft voice crackled under the pain of the loss of her mom, yet Collier went on to say: "You took something very precious from me. I will never talk to her again. I will never, ever hold her again. But I forgive you. And have mercy on your soul."[4]

Forgiveness builds and rebuilds the bridge hate and prejudice have attempted to destroy. Reconciliation is not a spectator's sport. You have to get into the game by actively helping to build or rebuild the multicultural bridge in your world.

Why Did the Samaritan Stop?

Have you ever wondered why the Samaritan stopped to help the wounded man? I have. Jesus was the storyteller. So, the story must align with the storyteller's values since He's trying to teach the hearers a life lesson. Jesus' story was all about this simple fact: proof of your conversion is shown through your ability and willingness to love your neighbor as yourself (Luke 10:27). The fact Jesus purposefully left out all racial and cultural identifiers of the wounded man helps us see that reconciliation is everyone's responsibility. We know the priest was Jewish. The Levite was also Jewish. The Samaritan, who we've come to call "The Good Samaritan," though unnamed, was not unidentified. The Samaritans were a group of people highly despised by the Jews. The race, culture, and ethnicity of these three characters were all identified. The fourth character, the wounded man, remains a mystery to us.

Why did the Samaritan stop? Perhaps he had pity on the wounded man because as a Samaritan he could easily relate to being mistreated and viewed negatively by society (John 4:9). We can't be 100 percent sure of this. What we can be sure of is: he stopped and he helped. He demonstrated that he loved the wounded man as he loved himself. Forgiveness will do that for you. It's empowering.

If you are going to build or rebuild a multicultural bridge you're also going to have to stop and inconvenience yourself the way the Samaritan did. And, in the same way the Samaritan's act cost him something, your extension of diversity has a price tag. It will cost you to practice this kind of love—a selfless love that cares equally for people across the great racial divide. Love is not color conscious. Eternal life gives you a new worldview—a godly outlook toward people and life in general. The Samaritan did not see love as a project. His love was pure, straightforward, and simple. His love said, "I have to stop and help. It's just the right thing to do. Period." Consider loving those you may have been estranged from because of past racial hurts so your life reflects Jesus' kind of love—one which, while costly, pays eternal dividends.

CHAPTER FIVE

Tolerance versus Accommodation

I think there's some truth to the stereotype that says, "Men and women shop differently." At least it is true in my relationship with Marlinda. When we first got married she said to me one afternoon, "Honey, let's go to the mall. I need to pick up a pair of blue shoes." I said, "Cool." In my mind she was going to shop "the right way," the way I've shopped my entire life. I am a hunter. I go into a store and hunt down a shirt or bag a pair of pants within a few minutes. It was always an in and out process. If I wanted a blue shirt, I looked only at the blue shirts. When I saw the one I liked I went immediately to the register, paid for it, and was on my way. That is shopping. At least that's how I shop, or should I say, the way I hunted.

I discovered Marlinda shopped as if she was on a safari—which meant we would be doing a lot of sightseeing and touring. Not only would we look for shoes, we would look at everything else in the store or windows.

We went to the first shoe store, and she tried on a pair of blue shoes. The price was right and the shoes fit perfectly. I was so happy. We'd bagged a pair of shoes in only a few minutes. I eyed the exit door to the mall. But to my surprise Marlinda told the salesperson, "I'm going to check out some other places. If I want them, I'll come back." I was shocked. I thought we were done. Boy, was I mistaken. This was just the beginning. We walked a mile, so it seemed, to the other end of the mall where there was a second shoe store. As we walked, I mean as we strolled, Marlinda stared in all the windows. She took in all the sights. I felt like a prisoner. I was forced to take them in, too.

When we finally arrived at the second shoe store, Marlinda went through the same drill, trying on a pair of blue shoes. And just like the previous pair, they fit her perfectly and the price was also good. Yet, again she told the salesperson, "No thanks. I'm still shopping."

At this point I became livid. Prior to this shopping trip, I assumed she was a fellow hunter—someone who shopped like me, quickly and intentionally. I found out the hard way Marlinda's style was nothing like mine. She was taking in a full excursion loaded with sensational visual experiences. I was so angry my hair stood up like Don King's. You know the boxing promoter whose hair stands straight up in the air like he's just been electrocuted? That was me in the mall that afternoon. When we reached the third store, I was so frustrated I whipped out my credit card willing to go into debt just to hurry up and get out of there. I was going to buy ten pairs of blue shoes if that would end the nightmare. I couldn't walk around going from store to store any longer. I hated this safari-style shopping. It was painfully long and drawn out.

Marlinda wasn't happy with my behavior that day. She felt devalued, diminished, and tolerated. Looking back, I can now see she was right. I acted like an immature and insensitive husband. I was making my dear wife struggle with feelings of tolerance. I was trying to change her style of shopping to fit mine, thinking my style was the only and best style. That's what a perspective of tolerance does. It diminishes the other person on a deep level.

Fast-forward years later; in the providence of God we had two daughters and no sons. I was forced to grow up. Plus, I was outnumbered. When my wife and daughters invited me to the mall I used to dread it. Then one day, I discovered I could take a book with me. I learned how to be accommodating by not rushing them or making them feel diminished while shopping. I'd simply take a seat outside the fitting room and read. Every now and then they would come out to ask my opinion on an item of clothing they were considering. I'd calmly look up from my book, smile, and say, "That looks great," or "Try something else." After thirty-three years of marriage, I learned to practice accommodation instead of tolerance. I'm still a hunter and my wife still goes on safaris. We didn't change one another, but we did learn how to accommodate one another. The same principle can easily apply to building strong cross-race relationships.

What's Your Target?

A tagline that secular society touts as positive and essential to multicultural success is being politically correct. Anything less will

One in Christ

bring you shame and ridicule for displaying intolerance toward people who are different from you. That's exactly what happened in 2017 when disgraced talk show host Bill O'Reilly joked he couldn't hear a word Congresswoman Maxine Waters was saying because of that "James Brown wig" she was wearing.[1] His off-the-cuff insult to the African American woman was quickly picked up by all the news outlets and labeled politically incorrect and intolerant. It's true that the way black women wear their hair has led to much discussion in the political and professional space. The fact that O'Reilly was using hair as a jab, a joke of sorts, struck a racial blow. To save face, O'Reilly, who happens to be white, released an apology a few hours after the segment aired. But it was too late. His apology was interpreted as disingenuous by people across the racial divide. Additionally, even his attempted cleanup did not work. It merely pointed to one of the flaws associated with political correctness. A lot of people who are politically correct are not cross-cultural nor do they aspire to be. They just want to function in a pluralistic environment as secret service operatives for monocultural living. O'Reilly's dig against the congresswoman brought that reality to the surface.

If you look at the flawed underpinnings of political correctness and intolerance from a slightly different perspective you may draw the same conclusion as Shelby Steele, professor at Stanford University. He said when people live up to the flawed definition of these terms they only "offer people a language through which they can console themselves with the feeling that they are superior to the nation's racial shame."[2]

The biblical aim behind multicultural relationships, whether inside or outside the church, is to provide solutions to a broken society (Matthew 5:13-14). Society is saddled with problems like racial prejudice, social injustice, limited opportunities for some groups, and the imbalance of power. Multiculturalism would balance the scales of power, provide a voice for the voiceless, and show equal concerns for all groups in our pluralistic society. Applying the biblical intent behind multiculturalism to the sectors of business and economics, family, and the Christian church should result in a stronger, more revitalized society operating within a more cohesive value system.

That's the target for Christians. This mark can only be achieved through the forging of personal cross-race relationships. Healthy cross-race relationships must be built on mutual respect, trust, and accommodation. We need to know how to speak with people of other cultures in respectful ways. That's why O'Reilly was labeled as politically incorrect and intolerant.

What's Tolerance?

In stepping away from O'Reilly's gaffe and cultural insensitivity we must ask ourselves a pointed question. Is tolerance good? I mean, if you *tolerate* those who are different than you, is that a good thing? The *Random House College Dictionary* defines *tolerance* as "allowing the right of something that one may not approve."[3] The English Oxford Living Dictionary gives us this definition of *tolerance*: "The ability or willingness to tolerate the existence of opinions or behaviour that one dislikes or disagrees with."[4] No matter the dictionary you consult and the various shades of meaning it offers you will see something consistent in every meaning of *tolerance* and *tolerate*. The definitions show there's a pointed negativity involved when you tolerate someone. To be tolerant of another is to say, "I prefer to not be around you. Having you in my space, my life, my world is not my preferred option."

Several years ago I was teaching a mid-week Bible study. The topic that night just happened to be on "Developing a Multicultural Lifestyle." There was a group exercise partway through the lesson. I had people pair up in groups of twos to seek answers to the questions I posed. After a few moments a Persian lady in the congregation, who I'd never met before, approached me privately requesting to be assigned a different partner. I asked why. She said, "I have nothing in common with my partner. She is a white woman and a former alcoholic, I just learned."

I asked her to accept this assignment as a growth opportunity, explaining to her it was important she learn to make accommodations for other people. She reluctantly accepted my response and continued with her original partner. Her question showed me that sitting next to the other lady for a ninety-minute Bible study was not too much of a disturbance. She could tolerate that with no problem. But, being asked to interact with her was asking too much. This is where she drew the line. Her tolerance level was reached. The thought of being together, at least in an exchange of ideas around a series of questions, was not something she was willing to put up with. This is a picture of tolerance. It's never positive in matters of relationships and will only "put up with" so much in interpersonal relationships.

Can you imagine how the other lady would have felt had she learned of her partner's feeling of tolerance toward her? She was being tolerated just by sitting next to the Persian lady, who felt talking to her was extreme. If this woman had gotten wind of how she was being tolerated it could have caused a cross-cultural riot. Our church would have received a black eye that night. And while it was only this Persian lady, and not all Persians, who had a problem of intolerance, the impact of her intolerance wouldn't have been felt any less by the congregation.

The pain of being tolerated cuts deep. It makes you assume things, false things, about yourself and others. Who knows what that lady would have thought that night had she learned someone was having a problem with her? Depending on her spiritual maturity, she may not have returned to our church again. A spiritually immature person tends to lump everyone from the same congregation into the same bucket if they've been offended. The pain of being tolerated would have caused the white woman to ask herself a series of questions, such as, "Why am I not welcomed at this church? What's wrong with me? Why do I feel ugly, repulsive, and devalued?" And, if those sentiments leaked out to the rest of the congregation, it would take quite some time to repair the damage.

Sadly, in some instances the pain can't be fixed in the setting where the offense occurred. It is particularly hurtful in a religious setting. A religious setting is supposed to be a safe space—a place where you can unburden your soul from the contamination of the world. A religious space is where you go to find solace, peace, and a comforting word from the Lord. It's not a place where you go to get abused, devalued, or simply tolerated. It is a place where you go to be understood and to find acceptance.

A Latina approached me a few weeks ago with tears streaming down her face. She was feeling discriminated against at her workplace. As a social worker who was given responsibility over a racially diverse district within her community, she was eager to serve the needs of the people. In her attempt to be thorough, she investigated the voicemail for the hotline reserved for callers who spoke only Spanish. Though this wasn't her assignment, she wanted to do a good job.

To her surprise the voicemail had not been checked for months. There were tons of messages left in the voicemail box. These were messages left by people in dire straits and they were reaching out to the agency for help. Some of the messages indicated the people in need had hard deadlines. Some were even suicidal. When she ran the problem up the chain of command the response shook her to the core. The leaders, all non-Hispanics, simply said, "Just delete the messages. We don't have time to go back over those calls."

You can imagine how she must have felt on hearing this callous response from her supervisors. When she shared her pain with me, any sign of tolerance on my part would have made matters worse. She turned to a church for help in sorting through the complicated emotions swirling inside her head and heart. We are commanded to love one another. We've been given an example of how to do that. Jesus is our example. The reason why tolerance is so negative and destructive is because at its core there is an element of self-love. Self-love focuses on one's own value, preferences, and desires above others. It conveys that you love yourself more than you love your neighbor. When self-love is present, it easily overlooks the ability to love others, especially those who don't look like you, believe what you believe, or speak English. Proof of discipleship is how we love one another.

Aware of how important my role was in encouraging and validating this woman, I first listened. I offered a biblical plan for how to remedy her problem as it related to her personal worth as a Latina. But I also pointed her to some ways to handle the work-related problem. The church should not tolerate people. We must accommodate them. She was most grateful for my pastoral guidance in this delicate matter.

What Is Accommodation?

People who want to establish a multicultural environment must practice accommodation. Accommodation says, "You matter to me. I want you in my life, so I will make room for our differences." This kind of an environment allows for our cultural differences. The major culture within a local faith community should not directly or indirectly force you to abandon your personal cultural identity and adopt theirs. Some groups do that and falsely label their community as multicultural. It's not. It's monocultural. Whenever a culture is made to conform to the culture of the majority, you're really dealing with a monocultural organization, family, community, or church. In a pluralistic society, one where multiple cultures and worldviews exist, most monocultural environments operate under the guise of tolerance and not accommodation when distilled to their cellular level.

The ministry leaders of the Antioch Church reflected a cross-cultural, multiethnic team. The Bible points out its diverse ethnicity and culture when it says, "Now in the church at Antioch there were prophets and teachers: Barnabas, Simeon called Niger, Lucius

One in Christ

of Cyrene, Manaen (who had been brought up with Herod the tetrarch) and Saul" (Acts 13:1).

From piecing together several Bible passages we learn Barnabas was a Jewish man, born and raised in the cross-cultural city of Cyprus (Acts 4:36). Simeon, called Niger, was an African, which we know from the meaning of his surname, "Niger." It means black. Lucius was a Greek, which we draw from the city he's associated with, Cyrene. Manaen was also a Greek. But the fact he was taken as a child to the ruler's court to be brought up with Herod as his foster brother adds a cultural twist to his persona. He knew how to walk among people who occupied the halls of power. The fifth leader, and the primary one in the Antioch Church, was Saul, who was also called Paul (Acts 13:9). Paul was a Hebrew brought up in the cross-cultural city of Tarsus.

These men had to be well-versed in the practice of accommodation to form and maintain such a diverse leadership team as this one. Each of these five leaders operated in his primary area of gifting. Together they were the eldership team of a powerful church. Each had to be impressive in his own right. That means each one had to know who he was and to be at peace with who he was and who he was not. Of equal importance was their ability to function alongside other powerful leaders without losing their identity or feeling overshadowed by another person's ability. Because the Antioch Church environment was accommodating, it was easy for these leaders, and I suspect the regular rank and file members, to come into their own. This is critical to achieve a cross-cultural expression. If someone is in a position of leadership or a place of visibility but lacks the necessary gifts to do an effective job, his placement will easily be interpreted as an act of tokenism. The

Antioch Church did not fall prey to this weakened approach to build a multicultural leadership team.

Trust, compromise, and respect are the three main ingredients to accommodation and each runs contrary to tolerance. Together, they form the powerful force of accommodation.

1. Trust

You cannot achieve a healthy relationship without the ingredient of trust. Be it a marriage, parental, or an employee-to-employer relationship, trust is the linchpin. Even our relationship with God is dependent on trust. We're told to *"Trust* in the Lord with all your heart and lean not on your own understanding; in all your ways submit to him, and he will make your paths straight" (Proverbs 3:5-6, italics mine). Trust means to place your confidence in someone or something. As Christians, if we don't place our confidence in God we will go astray. If there is no trust, we will abandon His leadership in our lives and surrender to our own ways, ways that have selfishness at their core.

In a cross-race relationship, trust must be present and fostered if that relationship is to survive. Trust says, "I believe you won't hurt me, because you have proven you care for me." Trust is earned. It is not automatically given just because you show up smiling or appearing to be well intentioned. Trust is not even given because you wear the title of Christian. Trust must be earned over time and over a series of encounters.

My first time preaching in Zambia left me with some concerns. I met the pastor of this large church a year earlier while I was on another speaking engagement in Africa. That time I was in Kenya speaking at an international leadership conference. He was also a guest speaker and we hit it off on many levels. He extended an invitation for me to come the following year to Lusaka, Zambia's capital. It was going to be a series of meetings with his congregation of ten thousand members. I was scheduled to address hundreds of his leaders on Friday and Saturday, and then speak to the broader congregation on Sunday.

Zambia is a very poor country especially in contrast to American standards. I was shocked to learn the exchange rate back then was 4,500 Zambian Kwachas to one American dollar. The country's poverty was compounded by the poor exchange rate. This led many of the people to be extremely sensitive toward visitors who came from abroad. Let me explain.

Much of preaching is intuitive. The preacher either feels connected or disconnected from his audience. After the first two times I spoke to the Zambian congregation I felt very disconnected. I felt as if they were guarded, even holding their breath for their negative suspicions to be confirmed by my sermon. After the second sermon I asked the pastor: "Am I misunderstanding what I'm feeling and sensing? I feel like your congregation is very guarded with me." His answer was startling. He said, "This is your first time in this part of Africa. My people don't know if you're going to hurt them. You're an American. They see you as rich and themselves as poor. They don't know if they can open their heart to your ministry yet."

I had to build trust with them. By the time I completed the last service on Sunday, the suspicion had lifted. I felt trusted. I earned their trust. Trust makes people open and vulnerable to your influence. The lack of trust closes them off much like a turtle withdraws into its shell as a protective act. Trust is critical in every relationship. If it's violated, it must be regained.

In cross-race relationships building trust can even be slowed if a major racial squabble breaks out in society. Although you had nothing to do with it, if your cross-race relationship does not have a strong foundation of trust, you may find the relationship pushed back two steps on the rung of trust because of an unrelated societal problem. Unrest on a national or regional level can create suspicion on a personal level. That's why you must always work at building and maintaining trust in your cross-race relationship.

From Scripture, "Trust in the Lord...and lean not on your own understanding," we learn that trust is built on the ability to lean on someone. God says we ought to lean on Him if we're going to demonstrate trust in Him. Your cross-race relationship will present opportunities for you to provide support to that other person. The support can come in the form of advice, emotional strength, laughter, friendship, or whatever strengths you bring to personal relationships. If there is a consistent benefit the other person receives from you and you from them, a bond of trust will naturally form. Trust is essential to creating the feeling of accommodation.

2. Compromise

Relationships that stand the test of time hold to the importance of compromise. Compromise means *"to come to terms, reach a settlement, a middle ground, or an understanding."* In essence, compromise is your willingness to make room for other peoples' lives to flourish, for their thoughts to be voiced, and for their gifts to find meaningful expression.

Compromise is the exact opposite of selfishness. Selfishness makes others small and you big. Compromise places the well-being of another on equal footing with yours. In a cross-race context, compromise sends a strong message. It says, "My way is not the only way of doing things or even seeing things." Compromise takes the expression of God in others into account.

One of the greatest things I've ever done is to follow through on my wife's idea to start a creative team. Our creative team is comprised of about a dozen people who have a unique perspective on learning styles, ministry methods, and how to bring an illustrative approach to my sermons.

I present my sermon calendar to the team leader and pastor of creative arts, Marco Hernandez, who holds a master's degree in fine arts and is the consummate artist. Previously, he built displays for the Bronx City Children's Museum before joining the staff at Christ Church. Each member of the creative team provides a different perspective of creativity to help dramatize the big idea behind each sermon. We build on each other's ideas and suggestions. Some team members have strong personalities, while others are on the quieter side. Over time we've learned the quiet folks are deep thinkers. They need to be called upon to share their ideas even though we have a free-for-all process. When they speak, the loud mouths among us, including me, keep quiet so they don't feel stifled or unimportant to the discussion. I'm not suggesting the team is perfect or operates like a well-oiled machine all the time. What I'm saying is we've learned the value of compromise in producing great ideas.

In any relationship each person must be allowed to speak and make a contribution in keeping with his or her S.H.A.P.E. Pastor Rick Warren devised this beautiful acronym to help people discover how God has uniquely designed them so they can make a positive contribution wherever they're planted. The letter S in the word

SHAPE represents "spiritual gifts." The H stands for "heart." The letter A refers to "ability" while the P stands for "personality." And, the letter E represents "experiences." When you allow the people in your sphere to function based on their SHAPE, you will have a wealth of benefits—personally and professionally.

You can easily measure the effectiveness of your ability to create an environment of compromise by how well people are functioning based on their SHAPE. If they are making a good contribution, it's because you've made room for them to function based on their SHAPE. You've allowed a healthy sense of compromise to exist in your relationships. Everyone wins when compromise exists.

3. Respect

Another critical ingredient in any relationship, including the cross-racial one, is respect. Paul tells us respect is essential to every marriage. He writes, "...and the wife *must respect* her husband" (Ephesians 5:33, italics mine). Here the word *respect* means *"to be in awe, to treat with deference."* In a marriage, a husband interprets the wife's display of respect as: "she loves me." In a cross-race relationship the other person interprets your actions of respect as, "I'm valued. I'm accepted."

Respect is evident and felt when each person voluntarily accepts the other. When you're respected, your input and opinion are sought. An environment of respect causes you to open up and connect on a deep emotional level with the people around you. When disrespect is the 800-pound gorilla in the room, you will shut down verbally and recoil emotionally. You won't offer any advice or opinions even though you have the answer that can solve the other person's problem. Disrespect breeds anger and resentment. On the other hand, respect breeds consideration and thoughtfulness. The more you are respected, the more you feel a sense of belonging and can demonstrate a willingness to contribute positively to the welfare of the relationship.

A major debacle many of the southern states are facing is the placing of Confederate icons in the market square of a multiethnic America. The people opposed to their removal cry, "You can't change history!" And they are absolutely correct. No one can change history. But if we want to achieve social harmony and establish healthy multiethnic relationships, we must ease the pain of those in our midst who've been hurt by historical wrongs. One surefire way of facilitating healing is to demonstrate consideration and thoughtfulness for how they feel. Removing the icons from the marketplace and placing them appropriately in museums will help to maintain a connection to history without causing harm to those whose ancestors were victims in history.

We cannot stand behind our social bully pulpits and demand the Confederate icons remain in a celebrated public space while in the same breath ask the question, "Why can't we all get along?" It won't work. It smacks of hypocrisy.

When I was in grad school, I visited the apartment of a friend who was an international engineering student from Colombia. He was married and had two little children. His family was here with him while he was completing his master's degree. I was a single guy, and I couldn't help noticing a leather strap with a wooden handle prominently hung on the doorframe between the kitchen and the living room. It was almost six feet off the ground. I was curious as to the meaning and our friendship was strong enough for me to ask my question. So, I asked, "What's the strap about?" He said, "To keep my kids in line, I point to the strap. They know if my wife or I take it down they'll receive a spanking for misbehaving." The strap was a reminder of past spankings, and it reinforced a certain desired behavior. If I was one of the children living in that home, I wouldn't like it. The strap would not only create fear in my heart, it would confuse my motivation to obey my parents. I'd have to ask myself, "Am I being driven by love or motivated by fear?"

Although it's not quite the same, Confederate icons remind African Americans of a not- too-distant past in which social injustices reigned. In every period of American history, including the period surrounding the Confederate era, there are things we can point to that were good even though they accompanied bad things. However, for the sake of reconciliation, perhaps moving those icons deemed good by some to a more fitting space is more appropriate. As a society we must wrestle with these kinds of tough questions, while also keeping our eye on the target of achieving healthy cross-race relationships. In other words, pain delays healing. Pain also adversely affects our behavior. Unresolved conflict slows the healing process and adversely affects our future opportunities.

Sally, a woman in her thirties, agreed to go out on a Friday night date with a man named Michael. He was to pick her up at her home at 7:00 p.m. At 7:30 p.m. Michael was still not there and he didn't call to say he'd be late. He pulled up at 7:35 with a big smile across his face. The moment Sally heard the doorbell, she flung open the door and blasted him with a barrage of anger-filled words, reading him the riot act. She told him off and ended with this, "No man is going to disrespect me!" At that, she slammed the door in his face.

Michael was shocked at what just happened. He never had the chance to explain he'd gotten into a little fender bender on his way to her house. He timed his arrival for 6:45 p.m. but the accident threw everything off. And because he was so nervous about making a good impression with Sally he rushed out of his house without his cell phone. Sally was so angry she made a hasty and incorrect assumption about Michael. The problem was not simply her assumption. The real problem was Michael became the whipping boy for all the men in Sally's past who disrespected her. When Sally angrily said, "No man is going to disrespect me" she was communicating, "I need to be healed."

So often, your past is the biggest hindrance to forming healthy cross-race relationships. The people who disrespected or devalued you yesterday because of your race, gender, culture, or whatever, are still holding you back today. Though they may be nowhere to be found, they are still with you emotionally and psychologically.

Respect is about you taking note of someone else's worth. It's about placing the other person's value on the same tier as yours. When that occurs, you will always have an opportunity to build a relationship based on honesty and vulnerability.

Accommodation Beats Tolerance Any Day!

Tolerance reflects judgment while accommodation exhibits grace. Judgment says you must change to be accepted. Grace says I accept you the way you are. Tolerance focuses inwardly on my awkward feelings about you, how I don't like the way you are, the way you act, etc. Accommodation focuses outwardly on others. It wants to know others are doing well and are feeling accepted.

Tolerance reflects impatience in the relationship while accommodation reflects patience. Tolerance says, "I really don't want a relationship with you." Accommodation says, "I want a relationship with you. I want you in my life." Tolerance reflects the old life—the life before salvation, where self is on the throne. Accommodation shows the new life—the life after salvation, where Christ is on the throne. Tolerance divides while accommodation unites. Tolerance is racially unattractive, but accommodation is racially attractive.

Accommodation is possible if you've been changed by Christ. Seek to live a life of accommodation. That kind of life will always prove attractive across racial and cultural lines.

CHAPTER SIX

Healthy Cross-Race Friendships

Every now and then a single Facebook post meant to keep your small social circle up to speed with the happenings in your life takes a wider turn and goes viral. That's exactly what happened when Lydia Rosebush posted a picture of her son, Jax, standing next to his best friend, another five-year-old little boy, Reddy Weldon, after a haircut. These inseparable friends were showing off their similar hairdos. Days earlier, Jax was told he needed a haircut because his hair was too long and out of control. He agreed. But he made a special request to his mom, that his hair be cut really low like Reddy's. This was Jax's reason: "He said he couldn't wait to go to school on Monday with his hair like Reddy's so that his teacher wouldn't be able to tell them apart,"[1] his mother said.

The Internet blew up because when Lydia posted the picture on Facebook, everyone saw what the two little boys didn't see. Jax was white and Reddy was black. Yet they were certain their preschool teacher would mistake the one for the other because their crew cuts would make them look identical. The story became a media frenzy. Why? I suspect it touted a model of what a healthy cross-race friendship looks like.

The fact the Internet blew up because of this small example of a strong interracial friendship is proof positive the world is craving such examples. It is as if people want to have cross-racial friendships, but they just don't know how to go about forming and developing them. This is where the church should come in. In a divided society the church must function as a working model of unity. Unity, particularly the cross-cultural kind, is attractive. It invites others to follow suit.

This is why Jesus emphatically said, "Let me give you a new command: Love one another. In the same way I loved you, you love one another. This is how everyone will recognize that you are my disciple—when they see the love you have for each other" (John 13:35, The Message).[2] This command was not uttered for a select few to live up to; it is expected for you and me to obey it. Your family and friends need a role model to show them how they ought to develop and maintain healthy cross-race friendships. You're it. That is what Jesus said.

The Marks of True Friendship

Since my 1986 supermarket experience, when I felt God commission me to address the question of diversity in the church, I have worked hard to understand how cross-race friendships are formed and maintained. In fact, my doctoral dissertation was specifically on black-white relationships in large multiracial churches. I wanted to learn what caused multiracial churches to form and how they maintain their diverse makeup. After traversing America to interview black and white senior pastors who lead multiracial churches, conducting dozens of focus groups, and analyzing reams of surveys completed by members of racially mixed congregations, I discovered the answers to two major questions. First, how do you build healthy cross-race friendships? Second, how do you build strong cross-cultural churches? The second question will be addressed in chapter eight, but we'll tackle the first question in this chapter.

I gathered and analyzed thousands of surveys from eight multiracial congregations from across the country. I also conducted about two dozen focus groups—two per congregation. Each focus group had ten to twelve participants. If the senior pastor of that congregation was black, the focus groups from his church included only whites. Similarly, if the lead pastor of a congregation was white, the focus groups from that church consisted of just blacks. There were other technical anchors established to ensure the research method and analysis would stand up to academic scrutiny.

I was amazed there were thousands of healthy multiracial relationships that had stood the test of time. These cross-race relationships weathered life's major milestones, including the marriage or divorce of their friends, the births and untimely deaths of children, graduations, job promotions, and employment terminations. These friendships even weathered societal storms like the 1992 Los Angeles race riot that resulted from the excessive use of force by the Los Angeles police in the arrest of Rodney King—the African

American man who tried to calm down the riot with the now infamous line: "People, I just want to say, you know, can we all get along?"[3]

The fact that these cross-cultural relationships survived personal and public storms is a wonderful indicator that such relationships can and do exist. Whether they knew it or not, these individuals applied eight building blocks in establishing their healthy cross-race friendships. While each building block may not be at work, most must be evident for a cross-race relationship to be considered a healthy one that lasts. The eight building blocks can either be categorized as actions or attitudes, and each category is characterized by four items. The following table details where things fell.

Eight Building Blocks for Healthy Cross-Race Friendships			
	Required Attitudes		Required Actions
	Demonstrate comfort in the relationship.		Offer hospitality.
	Be free to laugh and joke.		Engage in vulnerable conversations.
	Practice honesty in the relationship.		Go on social outings.
	Seek mutually rewarding outcomes.		Have cross-race friends.

Required Attitudes

Attitude reflects the disposition, perspective, and the approach a person takes when attempting to foster and develop a cross-race friendship. In many instances the attitude taken is organic, and not intentional at all. It simply became a reality in the relationship and proved a significant reason for the health and success of the relationship. Attitude is often silent, but its impact comes across very loudly in social situations. If your attitude is friendly, warm, and authentic, it draws people into your life. They want to get to know you, and for you to get to know them.

If your attitude is standoffish, antisocial, or dispassionate, you will repel people. They will be unimpressed with you. And certainly, that is not what people do who want to attract and build cross-race friendships. Fortunately, you can learn how to develop the same attitude over time and therefore achieve the same success in any budding cross-race relationship you're involved in.

1. Demonstrate comfort in the relationship.

I was amazed to see how person after person, independent of one another, described the comfort they felt in forming their cross-race relationships. It's very much the same effortless style Jesus portrayed when He spoke with the Samaritan woman at the well (John 4). The woman pointed out their ethnic differences when she said, "'You are a Jew and I am a Samaritan woman. How can you ask me for a drink?' (For Jews do not associate with Samaritans.)" (John 4:9). Jesus didn't answer her. He wanted to build a rapport with her that would lead to a bigger payoff than simply getting a cup of water. He wanted her soul to be saved. For that to occur, she needed to feel comfortable in the relationship. And it worked.

Jesus' approach to the woman began with His being comfortable with her. He wasn't awkward in her presence. And, despite their ethnic differences, He created a rapport that helped her not to feel awkward around Him. Clearly, they were different. The woman said He was a Jew. I'm sure His features and possibly His clothing gave that away. Part of Jesus' ability to make her feel comfortable was He did not draw attention to her ethnicity. He didn't say, "I have no problem talking with Samaritan women." His approach to her sent that signal.

The people with cross-race friendships in the focus groups I conducted spoke with ease about their formation. For some folks, their cross-race friendship was the first one they'd ever had. In other words, they weren't experts in diversity. They were just people who were willing to open their hearts to someone else. They didn't bring up the other person's race, culture, or ethnicity for frivolous reasons. When people do that, it creates a tangible discomfort and reduces the probability of a cross-race relationship forming.

When someone says, "My Chinese co-worker got a good deal on four snow tires last week. I'm going to check out the same tire store next week," a red flag goes up, alerting those he's speaking to that the racial difference is meaningful. But there's no reason to mention the co-worker's ethnicity. First, it doesn't add to the story. And second, it doesn't clarify any portion of the story. This kind of statement only serves to highlight your lack of cross-cultural awareness. Anyone from a different race or culture who hears you make that statement will find it awkward. They'll also interpret it to mean when they are not in your presence you tell similar stories using their ethnicity as an identifier in the same meaningless way.

It points to not only ignorance on your part, but also to your possible discomfort.

In the 1970s a popular television show called *All in the Family* had a main character, Archie Bunker, who constantly labeled people based on their ethnicity. One of the reasons the show was so successful, I believe, was because the shock value of Archie's ignorant name-calling generated awkward chuckles. It was a time in American history when bigotry was becoming less acceptable in mainstream culture. And hearing Archie Bunker speaking that way was a comical way of making the point painfully apparent that this kind of behavior was unacceptable.

You can't fake being comfortable, at least not for any extended period. And no one wants to force the development of a new relationship. It's an awkward, painful, and distasteful process. If you have nothing in common with the other person, your relationship will lack the ingredients to make it grow. In same-race relationships and certainly in cross-race relationships people spend time with those who make them feel comfortable.

2. Be free to laugh and joke.

People-watching is both educational and entertaining. You learn quite a bit about human nature—the good, the bad, and the ugly. One thing you quickly observe is the role comfort plays in people being themselves. People clam up when they don't feel comfortable because they don't know how they'll be received. That's why strangers are often stiff and reserved when they first meet. The moment they become comfortable with each other they start to loosen up. Their real personality surfaces and jokes and laughter can be heard.

My friend Ylonda has a friend whose dad is Jewish and mother is East Indian. When he meets people at parties, he often says, "People always want to know how I got a name like Emil Rosenberg—simple, I'm HinJew." Emil's line always gets a laugh. That's because Emil is being his natural self when he jokes around. If you're not funny, don't attempt to be funny especially when you're trying to develop a new relationship. You will be viewed as someone who's trying to mask your cross-cultural discomfort with jokes, and bad ones at that. In the same breath, don't become a clown even if you are naturally comedic. Clowns are for entertainment. You're trying to build a true relationship—one that includes courtesy, care, and an opportunity to share your life with someone else.

What I have observed is when people are relaxed, truly relaxed around others, even people of other races, they allow their true personalities to surface. Laughter and joking is a major part of American culture. As you are forming cross-race relationships even this ingredient, as minor as it may seem, plays a critical role. It sends a signal that says, "You are safe with me. And you'll even have a good time hanging out with me. I'm comfortable with you."

3. Practice honesty in the relationship.

Trust is one of the most critical building blocks in any relationship. Trust says, "You've been honest with me. Therefore, I can trust you." This discovery came to light as I probed the participants who described the glue that held their cross-race friendships together. Honesty was a recurring theme when they described the feelings they held for their friends. It wasn't any one thing the friend did. It was more of a feeling formed over time and over the course of many interactions.

Another word came up frequently in the focus groups when I asked participants to tell me what they meant by *honesty*. That word was *credibility*. Their cross-race friends proved to be credible with them. When someone demonstrates credibility toward you, you know where you stand with him. Whatever he says to your face is the very thing he says behind your back. The converse is equally true. Whatever he says to others about you when you're not around is pretty much what he says to your face. This kind of relational honesty is not only refreshing, it's encouraging. You're encouraged to open more of your social life to that person. You feel safe with him. And, assuming this person feels the same sense of emotional safety about you, the relationship is sure to take off.

I remember many years ago I was to meet this husband and wife for marital counseling. We didn't even get a chance to exchange any social pleasantries before the husband angrily asserted, "My wife is a liar!" At that, his wife hung her head. She was embarrassed. And he was intentionally trying to embarrass her, especially in front of me. I had been their pastor for a number of years. I knew who they were. I also knew he could be a bit of a bully because of his domineering personality and style. Without thinking or measuring my words, I shot back: "She's a liar because of you!" A shocked look came across his face. Her head rose. They both waited for my explanation. I didn't disappoint them.

I told the husband his domineering and judgmental style contributed to her lying. She was afraid of being corrected and reprimanded because of how it was done. To avoid his tongue-lashings, she lied. The wife chimed in and said, "That's exactly why I lie. You're too harsh with me. It hurts!" A startled look came across his face as she went on to describe how his demeanor affects her truth-telling. That day, the husband got it. He finally connected the dots to see his wife was not a bad person, she was just fearful of his angry tone. He made a commitment to change, as did she, because there is really no excuse for lying.

The story illustrates how important honesty is in developing relationships. If people don't feel they can be themselves with you by telling you how they honestly feel, that is not good. In the early or even in the advanced stages of your cross-race friendships, don't be afraid to invite the person to correct you if you missed cultural cues or have offended him or her by your limited experience with diversity. Inviting correction is a surefire way to practice honesty in the relationship.

4. Seek mutually rewarding outcomes.

Healthy cross-race friendships are those built on equal social footings. Each person must be made to feel he shares the same social status as the other. The moment you think, and your actions support the thought, that you stand on a higher rung on the social ladder, the relationship will begin to disintegrate. It may also morph into a paternalistic or a maternalistic one, both of which are unhealthy models of cross-race relationships. Any top-down relationship weakens the peer concept, which is essential to a social, cross-race friendship.

Imagine a teacher-student relationship in a social space. I'm not speaking about matters of diversity here. I'm simply addressing the dynamic of relationship between a teacher and his or her student. The student automatically sees the teacher as an advisor, instructor, or go-to-person in a particular subject area. The teacher also sees the student as a learner who the teacher helped form, shape, and develop. The only way this dynamic can truly change is when the student earns the same or greater accomplishment as the teacher in that field or when something occurs to elevate the student's social status in an irrefutable way.

When I completed my Ph.D., I bumped into a former professor of mine and immediately addressed him as "Dr. So-and-so." Knowing of my recent academic accomplishment, he said, "From now on call me Craig. We're peers." He leveled our social playing field. It was no longer a top-down or bottom-up relationship but a peer-to-peer relationship, and I must admit, it made me feel great to hear him say that to me.

Relating to people socially can be tricky. There are lots of unspoken rules that affect us both consciously and subconsciously. Any feelings of cultural or racial superiority or inferiority towards members of other groups must be identified and brought to the Cross. If you feel superior to members of another race, you will take on a paternalistic view in your emerging cross-race relationship. You will unconsciously seek to guide, advise, or assume the greater level of influence in the relationship. This behavior can creep in, especially if members of your race have played that role historically.

To avoid falling prey to this dangerous social pitfall, always watch and pray. Watch your behavior, word choices, and the responses you get from people across the racial divide. If they tend to clam up or express inhibition and reserve by their lack of openness or laughter, it may mean you are assuming a top-down view of the relationship—and you're the one on top. If you observe any sign of this socially offensive behavior, recognize you must change. If you have a blind spot in this area, one way to experience change is through the influence of the Holy Spirit.

Peter had a top-down view toward Gentiles and he wasn't even aware of it. Everything came to a head after he had a powerful vision from God (Acts 10:9–22). The vision confronted his prejudice toward non-Jews. Peter's first opportunity to interact with a Gentile after his vision was to share Christ with Cornelius, a Roman soldier, in Cornelius' house. The home was packed with Cornelius' relatives and friends and other Gentiles. After Peter came in and got comfortable, he said: "I now realize how true it is that God does not show favoritism but *accepts* men from every nation who fear him and do what is right" (Acts 10:34–35, italics mine). It took a revelation from God, in response to his prayerfulness (Acts 10:9), for Peter to see his blind spot.

Don't be afraid to pray about your heart toward others. Don't be afraid to pray about your need to grow as a cross-cultural ambassador of the kingdom of God. God invites our prayers—even for help with forming cross-cultural relationships. Peter admitted his previous view before the heavenly vision was flawed and limited. He perceived those outside of his Jewish social circle as unimportant, less than, and of little value even to God. That attitude had to change if he was going to have any multicultural influence as a Christian. He had to change. Once change occurred, Peter sought a mutually rewarding outcome for Gentiles. He was aware they, too, were accepted by God. Social equality puts everyone on the same footing.

Required Actions

Our actions communicate our attitudes and feelings toward other people. If we don't like them, we tend to avoid them. If we like them, we find ways to connect with them. That's exactly what my research findings revealed about healthy cross-race friendships. In fact, there were four distinct actions that bolstered their cross-race friendships. These actions were not calculated or part of a strategic plan. They were just natural, organic, and a normal reaction of people who liked hanging out with each other regardless of their racial differences. By forming an awareness of what works to cement these kinds of relationships, you can take immediate action toward getting a leg up in your development of healthy cross-race friendships.

1. Offer hospitality.

When you are comfortable with someone of another race, offering that person some form of hospitality comes naturally. A surefire way to increase the strength of your friendship is to invite your friends to your home for a meal. I realize we live in a fast-paced, busy world. Our lives are extremely busy. We're so busy we hardly have time for our extended families and they share the same race. This is why taking time out of your life to host a small get-together at your home can be quite impactful.

You don't have to guess where someone's heart is when you're sitting at his or her dining room table. You made the cut. You're part of the gang. This person is comfortable sharing a social circle and private space with you. You didn't invite yourself. That person invited you.

Offering hospitality also offers you the opportunity to sample someone else's cultural food or music. When you're invited to enter someone's cultural space—be it an ethnic restaurant, a wedding, or some other social function—it's someone's way of opening another section of his or her life to you. Hospitality is an action undergirded by feelings of friendship, love, and care. When the opportunity presents itself, take it. The relationship will be strengthened because you reciprocated the gesture of friendship. When Peter accepted Cornelius' invitation and entered his home, it meant permission was granted for him to partake of a deeper part of the Gentile's life. That's what hospitality does.

2. Engage in vulnerable conversations.

We all have myths, suspicions, and unsupported ideas about members of other races. If these myths are not overturned, it means you'll go about your life with these legends in your mind, allowing them to silently influence you. One of the surprising facts my research unearthed was people who had healthy cross-race relationships were secure enough in their relationships to have vulnerable conversations with their friends.

Ron, a white guy, asked his friend, Derrick, an African American, about "the talk" black fathers had with their sons to avoid police brutality. With the advent of the cell phone and social media, our society is seeing instances where a heavy-handed approach by a few rogue police officers was taken against people of color. Black and Latino parents often speak to their sons about how to avoid getting into unnecessary confrontations with members of law enforcement. No longer wanting to walk around with thoughts that were myths or stereotypes, Ron approached Derrick.

These two men had been friends for years. Derrick was not offended, uncomfortable, or made to feel he was giving away secrets from his race. He answered Ron's questions candidly and honestly. The two guys spoke for well over an hour on the topic before they moved on to a lighter conversation. The fact that this type of vulnerable conversation is common in healthy cross-race friendships helps prepare both parties to be used by God to put out racial fires.

Accuracy of knowledge regarding cultural diversity allows you to de-escalate anger and racially tense circumstances. This is critical to flourishing in a multicultural society. In fact, as I write this chapter, a member of my staff just shared that she was invited to attend a pilot course on Cultural Diversity and De-Escalation offered by our state government. This is becoming commonplace in America, and it will become more so in the future because we're browning as a nation. Ethnic diversity is on the rise. Vulnerable conversations help dispel the unconscious biases, suspicions, and myths people have held toward each other for generations. I encourage you to deepen the bond of your cross-race relationship by gingerly broaching topics that can lead to vulnerable conversations. This step will anchor your relationship in the areas of comfort and honesty.

3. Go on social outings.

Friends do things together. They like each other's company. If you claim to be friends with your coworker, fellow church member, or whomever, and yet never spend time enjoying social outings with them, the authenticity of your cross-race friendship is in question.

While lounging around our living room after a Thanksgiving dinner, my youngest daughter, Jessica, shared that when she goes out with her friends, they teach her how to say her name in their mother tongue. She continued, "I know how to say, 'My name is Jessica,' in six different languages." Immediately she rattled off the phrase in Italian, Korean, German, Spanish, and Chinese. I then asked her, "Which Chinese language was that?" She said, "Mandarin." Her aunt Paula then asked, "Can you say it in Cantonese?" Jessica replied, "My Chinese friends only speak Mandarin." I smile when I recall this brief family moment because it points to the fact my daughter enjoys regular social outings with her cross-race friends.

Social outings give you and your friends the opportunity to experience things together. Find something you both enjoy and do it together. This will deepen your personal relationship while allowing you to influence the public on the reality that healthy cross-race friendship can and do exist.

4. Have cross-race friends.

Did you know having cross-race friends is contagious in that it leads to having more cross-race friends? Jesus puts it this way: "For everyone who has will be given more, and he will have an abundance" (Matthew 25:29). Although this statement was made at the tail end of the Parable of the Talents, Jesus was emphasizing to His disciples they had stewardship responsibility in the proper management of money and whatever else God placed in their lives. We must include the proper management of our relationships as part of our responsibility before the Lord.

Even if you're without any cross-race friendships and you're feeling a bit discouraged, let me settle your nerves. You can start from right where you are in building your first healthy cross-race friendship. Let me tell you how Phyllis, a white woman, and Louise, a black woman, became best friends. Phyllis grew up in an all-white community in the hills of West Virginia. She told me, "Not only were there no other races around us, but my father was also the consummate bigot, just like Archie Bunker. My dad would warn me to stay away from them whenever he saw people of different races during our monthly trips to the big city. 'They are no good,' he'd say. 'All they do is complain about whites hurting them or not giving them a fair shake.'"

The first time she had to be around an African American was when she began working. The coworker, Louise, was friendly, but Phyllis remained guarded and suspicious. Even though she was a Christian at that point, her father's poison was still in her system. She went on to say, "As I settled into the job, I knew I had to tell at least one person that I was battling neurocardiogenic syncope, a disease that caused me to pass out at any time for no apparent reason. Due to periodic low blood circulation to the brain, the disease would cause seizure-like symptoms and fainting spells," Phyllis explained. "This would even happen sometimes when I was driving. It was quite dangerous. Without anyone else to confide in, I turned to Louise and told her about my illness and what to do if that ever happened at work. She sympathetically listened and smiled, saying, 'God and I will help you, sweetheart.'"

About three weeks later, Phyllis was sitting in the conference room next to Louise when she passed out and slumped over the chair, immobile. When she came to, she was sitting in the emergency room with Louise and the doctors looking down on her. Louise had sprung into action and called 911. An ambulance whisked Phyllis off to the hospital. With tears welling up in her eyes, Phyllis said, "Louise, my first African American friend, saved my life." Their friendship continued to blossom from there. They went shopping together and ate dinner at each other's homes with their families.

This occurred over twenty years ago. Since then, Phyllis' pool of friends has come to look like the United Nations. And like Phyllis, you must start somewhere. But you don't have to stay there. If you want to thrive in building cross-race friendships, you can rest assured cross-race friends will lead to having more cross-race friends. For these friendships to grow and become mutually rewarding, don't forget to apply the appropriate attitudes and actions that lead to their healthy growth in your life.

CHAPTER SEVEN

Becoming an Authentic Reconciler

One of the most popular music programs on television nowadays is *The Voice*. This competition-based reality show is quite interesting because of the many sensational twists it presents. Right off the bat, you're drawn in because four prominent pop stars serve as judges. They sit in large red chairs with their backs facing the contestants. The judges cannot see the person who's singing; they can only hear them. If they like what they hear and believe that person has the potential to win the overall contest with a little coaching, they will press their buzzer. This signifies they want to be the person's coach throughout the competition. The part that intrigues me most is that the judges cannot choose someone based on their looks, race, age, or even gender. The singer's voice is the only thing the judges have to go by. As you know, the singer's voice oftentimes does not match their looks. Having their backs to the singer removes the bias.

I wanted to create a similar red-chair experience for you. Have you noticed it? Up to this point in the book, I have been silent about my race or ethnicity though my picture appears on the book's jacket. I realized it would be virtually impossible to conceal my identity in the process of launching this book, but I wanted you to have as little bias as possible as I shared my thoughts, ideas, and research on cross-race relationships in the church. I did not want you to hear my written voice through a filter that may have misled or misdirected you. I created a dynamic in which you could hear me much like the judges on the *The Voice* hear the contestants. I wanted to be heard as an authentic reconciler and not as a black guy who happens to strongly believe in racial reconciliation. An authentic reconciler who has no ax to grind and no harbored anger toward others because of previous racial injustices is the most effective and authentic reconciler. Such a person is often approached by people of every race to mediate their racial conflicts. I wanted you to hear my voice from that standpoint. As human beings, we have been wired to form opinions and conclusions of others based on their race. I didn't want you to categorize me, so I shared my heart without disclosing my race. But now I am inviting you to turn your chair around and see who I am and how I've come to be an authentic reconciler.

When I was eight years old, my parents immigrated our family from Jamaica to the United States. Two years later they purchased a small home in Rosedale, Queens, a quiet suburb in the outskirts of New York City. Two weeks after our family moved in, five white teenage boys threw a Molotov cocktail into one of the bedroom windows of our new home—into my bedroom window. The gasoline bomb exploded, and I saw a wall of flames as the fire began to burn our house. I shouted to alert my family about the blaze. We all ran out of the house, frightened like never before.

I can still see the fire trucks pulling up and the firefighters scrambling to get the hoses so the fire could be quickly extinguished. It seemed like a lifetime before they turned on the water and brought the fire under control. Finally, the blaze was out. As it turned out, only minor damage was done to our house. But that night a fire of uncertainty, confusion, bewilderment, and anger toward white people was kindled in my heart.

The hatred toward my family did not stop there. We had to have around-the-clock police surveillance because of the death threats we received from white families within the community. The firebombing made the evening news and became the talk of the region. And even though the five white boys were caught just a few days later, they were released without being charged of any wrongdoing. The judge said it was just a childish prank. Imagine that. This criminal act of vandalism— attempted murder, arson, a hate crime, and the list goes on—was ignored by our criminal justice system.

This was the first time I ever experienced prejudice and I was troubled and confused by what happened. What had my family done wrong? Why were we hated? What had we done to deserve such treatment from total strangers? Although my parents were hurt and disillusioned, they sat us children down and instructed us this way: "Don't hate white people because of what these boys did." Their words didn't register with me.

To me, anger seemed the only appropriate response to the injustice done to my family. My so-called neighbors bombed our house. My so-called neighbors tried to kill me. They taught me to hate myself because I was black. They taught me I was not loved, not worth loving, and not even good enough to be tolerated. Racial prejudice was totally new to me. My small island nation did not prepare me for such things. I didn't know how to view myself as a black kid in a predominantly white culture, much less as a despised child. The family next door to us wouldn't even speak to us. They moved away within a month of our living there because they did not want to live next door to a "black family." As a result of these incidences, I did not grow up feeling the need to build cross-cultural relationships, nor did I recognize the need to love my neighbor as myself.

When I was twenty years old and away at college, something happened that changed all that. At 10:00 p.m. on July 6, 1982, I accepted Jesus Christ as my Lord and Savior. I prayed a simple prayer, which I later learned was the prayer of salvation. Alone in my dorm room, I simply said, "Lord, if You are real, come into my heart and change me." I had heard the gospel message from some Christian friends who shared Jesus with me for an entire year leading to that day. My conversion came on the heels of a one-year journey to understanding the meaning of life. I concluded there must be more to life than making money, marrying a pretty girl, and having a great career. Though I had none of those things at that time, I saw them as empty goals. Despite all my attempts to straighten out those foolish Christians who repeatedly shared their faith with me, I found myself joining them a year later.

What was really amazing, though, was that the prayer of salvation didn't merely heal my sin-sick soul; it also healed me of the pain of victimization. I emerged from my dorm room both as a new believer in Jesus and as a man healed of prejudice and confusion over how I would live and connect with others in our pluralistic and multicultural society. If God could heal me, He can heal anyone of any aspect of social pain. I soon discovered the medicine Christ used to heal and inoculate me from the disease of prejudice was His love. Jesus set me free to love. He empowered me to love Him, myself, and all my neighbors.

I find it ironic. God chose me to build a multiracial congregation. Me, a black man! Me, a victimized man! Paul was right when he said, "But God chose the foolish things of the world to shame the wise; God chose the weak things of the world to shame the strong" (1 Corinthians 1:27). If God can use me, and my painful past, to accomplish these social feats, He can heal and use anyone to do the same and more. Quite often though, the ones who've been affected the most are the very ones who lead the mission for reconciliation and racial healing. The call for diverse representatives from the whole church is great. Reconciliation is not a black issue, a white, Hispanic, or an Asian issue. It is God's issue articulated in the Word for the entire church.

My healing was instantaneous. Yet for many, healing from prejudice is a journey—a difficult one. The Christian church is a healing institution. This means we cannot ignore the need to heal those inside and outside our ranks even if we did not cause their pain. That is why Jesus' parable of the Good Samaritan was so powerful. This unnamed helper took it upon himself to see to it the wounded stranger was cared for and healed. You must do the same when you come across racially wounded victims lying within your sphere of influence.

Keep It Real!

God does not hide the dirty laundry in His church. The Antioch Church was multiethnic, but, when Apostle Peter visited, a problem began to surface. It became very apparent his behavior was divisive. Peter was not an authentic reconciler and he didn't even know it. He didn't know how to connect with others across the racial divide or how to maintain unity within the multiethnic blend of the members. Since he was quite famous and influential as a leader in the broader church, his personal struggles with prejudice had to be addressed openly and respectfully. They were adversely impacting the unity of the congregation.

Paul, the senior leader at the Antioch Church, addressed it head-on. Galatians 2:11–21 presents the entire exchange. This passage best captures the reason for the confrontation:

> When Cephas (Peter) came to Antioch, I opposed him to his face, because he stood condemned. For before certain men came from James, he used to eat with the Gentiles. But when they arrived, he began to draw back and separate himself from the Gentiles because he was afraid of those who belonged to the circumcision group. The other Jews joined him in his hypocrisy, so that by their hypocrisy even Barnabas was led astray. When I saw that they were not acting in line with the truth of the gospel, I said to Cephas in front of them all, "You are a Jew, yet you live like a Gentile and not like a Jew. How is it, then, that you force Gentiles to follow Jewish customs?" (Galatians 2:11–14)

Peter's social preference fell short of the biblical principle of loving your neighbor and valuing diversity. Paul's big issue was that Peter needed to become an authentic reconciler, or at best, stop dividing the Antioch congregation. His behavior, whether unconscious or conscious, had to change. If not, he could not continue his visit at their multiethnic congregation.

Looking back throughout my journey and pastoral career, I have discovered authentic reconcilers don't stumble into that label. They must make an informed choice to become one. There are four voluntary actions you must take to wear the label of authentic reconciler. These people have chosen to:

1. Place faith above ethnicity.
2. Take a personal path over peer pressure.
3. Practice advocacy over silence.
4. Model diversity permanently versus temporarily.

1. Place Faith above Ethnicity.

Paul did not base his argument on his personal opinion or preference. He knew Peter's stumbling blocks. Like Paul, Peter was Jewish. He grew up with a Jewish worldview that distanced him from Gentiles. In his mind, based on his entire upbringing, Gentiles were considered sinners. After accepting Christ as his Messiah, Peter still held Gentiles at a social distance, not knowing what to do or how to connect with them, even the Christian ones. The Bible teaches, "Therefore, if anyone is in Christ, he is a new creation, the old has gone, the new has come" (2 Corinthians 5:17). Although

Peter's spiritual conversion happened a while back, he still had no idea how to walk out the diversity piece.

Paul's argument focused on Peter's need to place his faith above his ethnicity. That is why he openly said to Peter, "We who are Jews by birth and not 'Gentile sinners' know that a man is not justified by observing the law, but by faith in Jesus Christ. So we, too, have put our faith in Christ Jesus that we may be justified by faith in Christ and not by observing the law, because by observing the law no one will be justified" (Galatians 2:15–16). Faith must cause you to live above the importance and value of your ethnicity. Paul's argument was wholly steeped in the Scriptures.

He was challenging Peter to choose the correct practice position around which to center his life. The choice is to either be Christocentric or ethnocentric. Christocentric means Christ is the center of your life. Jesus is the one who must be given center stage. If your ethnicity is the center of your life and the way you derive your purpose, you are not a fully devoted follower of Jesus Christ. You can't have two centers. And, as important as your ethnicity is to you, that can't be the centerpiece of your life. Not after you've experienced faith in Jesus Christ. If your ethnicity takes a seat on the throne of your life it means you are ethnocentric and you live to promote your ethnicity. It also means you support its causes above the cause of Christ. And, it says you submit more to the leaders who influence your ethnic group than you submit to Christ-honoring leaders who just happen to be of a certain ethnicity. If that's the case, you may need to be confronted like Peter was concerning the error of placing his ethnicity above his faith. For a Christian, the order of importance needs to be reversed. To this very end Jesus said, "Why do you call me, 'Lord, Lord,' and do not do what I say?" (Luke 6:46). Peter's priorities needed a serious realignment.

We've all made decisions about how we're going to live, whether consciously or unconsciously. But, if you want to be an authentic reconciler, you must double-check your choices in order to ensure your life is completely in alignment with the Word of God. In the end, it's not what you want or what I want; it's what God wants that counts. His Word captures His will. The will of God is for you to place your faith above your ethnicity!

Walking It Out

At a festive backyard barbecue, two men shared their personal stories of mistakes and triumphs with me. One man was white and the other African American. The men became good friends over the years because they shared a common past. They were cellmates in prison. Both made drug related wrong choices. Both accepted Christ as their Savior prior to their imprisonment, but their wrong choices with marijuana and crack cocaine led to expensive drug habits neither could afford except through robbery and other criminal activities. As they shared their stories with me, they focused on their healing and the joy of freedom—freedom in Christ and now freedom from prison.

When Ken, the black guy, was being placed in the cell, Frank, the white brother, had already been there for a year. Frank had his shirt off and the swastika tattooed on his chest was clearly visible. The moment Ken saw it, he demanded the guard place him in another cell. "We'll kill each other," he said. "Give me another cell. This guy hates black people!"

The guard ignored his complaints and walked away, leaving the two inmates to settle their grievances in the way prisoners so often do.

Frank quickly realized what caused Ken's irritation and said, "Hey, man, don't worry. I'm no longer the guy this swastika says I am. I'm a born-again Christian and love people of all races."

Ken was shocked. He quickly told Frank, "I'm born-again also."

As we ate our hamburgers at the barbecue that afternoon, both Frank and Ken told me how they sang worship songs together in their cell to celebrate their joy in Christ. Ken regularly played his guitar, and the two men lifted their voices in harmony to the Lord. I walked away from that cookout amazed once again at God. His powerful grace enters the darkest parts of our lives to rescue us from the sin of prejudice and to convert us into authentic reconcilers.

If God can use Frank and Ken to model reconciliation in prison, what excuse do we have for disobeying the call of Christ to build bridges to other cultures? We have none. Just as Frank was unable to change the tattoo of his past, we may not be able to change certain aspects of our pasts. But he was able to surrender to Jesus his heart of prejudice and racial isolation so the passions of an authentic reconciler could be birthed in him. We can do the same. The ability to live cross-culturally comes about only because we have intentionally surrendered ourselves to Jesus' challenge to model reconciliation—and to model it authentically you must place your faith above your ethnicity.

2. Take a Personal Path over Peer Pressure.

Peter needed to be confronted because his behavior demonstrated hypocrisy. He used to eat with the Gentiles, joining in the love feasts—meals that helped to deepen the members' bonds with one another, but then a visible and noticeable change occurred. When some of the Jewish believers came from the Jerusalem Church to Antioch, Peter began to draw back socially, succumbing to the peer pressure calling for cultural separation. Out of fear of criticism from his Jewish buddies (Galatians 2:12), Peter was yielding to the mob mentality of monocultural living. This was wrong. It showed a partial, insincere commitment to diversity.

This mindless choice of Peter's had its repercussions. Paul noted, "The other Jews joined him in his hypocrisy, so that by their hypocrisy even Barnabas was led astray" (Galatians 2:12). Because of Peter's stature, his behavior was influencing other Jews who were members of the Antioch Church. Please understand. The Jews who came up from Jerusalem on a temporary visit created a social tension for Peter. Apparently, at that juncture in history, his multicultural footings and commitment were weak. He wanted to save face with these men by exclusively hanging out with them. To do that, he discontinued his socializing and eating with the Gentiles from the Antioch Church. His actions were so noticeable some of the other Jews, existing members of the Antioch Church, started doing the same thing. Even Barnabas, an elder in the Antioch Church, succumbed to this divisive, hypocritical behavior. You can see why Paul had to confront it head-on and publicly.

Monocultural vs. Multicultural Ministry

A monocultural church is wholly different than a multicultural one. In a multiethnic, multicultural church, knitted relationships are the glue that keeps the congregation united. When you drill

down, you will learn the preaching style in a monocultural ministry caters to one type of audience. It's not like that in the multicultural setting. In fact, if you're going to thrive in the racially diverse
church you must adopt the perspective that Ignatius of Antioch,
one of the early church fathers, taught. "In his view Christ is the
invisible supreme head, the one great universal bishop of all the
churches scattered over the earth. The human bishop is the centre
of unity for the single congregation, and stands in it as the vicar of
Christ and even of God."[1]

Ignatius recognized the difficulty we human beings have to
achieve unity in the local and universal church. Therefore, he urged
the believers to align themselves with their local pastor (also known
as vicar in some branches of the Church) as he aligned himself with
Jesus—the shepherd of the whole Church. Assuming the local pastor is multicultural in his ministry, as Jesus taught us to be, we in
turn would have a multicultural worldview.

In other words, when you are really teaching God's unadulter-
ated Word, it should not have a dogmatic slant. Whether a nation-
alistic, denominational, cultural, or racial slant, it shouldn't veer
off biblical tracks. You should be able to preach the same essential
message in Europe, South America, or Asia. You must be able to
speak to the whole world from your pulpit. Peter didn't understand
he had to forge a personal path, rather than conducting himself
based on peer pressure or the party line mantra of a few monocultural Jews.

The monocultural church is largely different than the multicultural one. Just observe the worship and you'll see a clear difference.
Monocultural worship only considers its monocultural audience
and their musical palate. Whereas in the multiethnic church, a wide

genre of music must be considered and used to serve its broader constituency. The biggest difference between the two types of churches is when misunderstandings occur. In the monocultural church, interpersonal conflicts are never viewed as racial or cultural issues, just as personality clashes. It's not like that in the multiethnic fellowship.

Misunderstandings and interpersonal conflicts can be viewed as being racial or cultural issues and not just a dynamic of a personality clash. And honestly, this creates a whole other set of problems. In the multiethnic church, we have to really know how to search for the real problem because immature people label everything as being racial when oftentimes race has little or nothing to do with the real issue.

Peter's behavior was unconsciously moving the Antioch congregation to a monocultural church model and that was not who they were or wanted to be. Paul stopped it dead in its tracks. He wanted everyone who called the Antioch Church a spiritual home to feel a genuine sense of belonging and acceptance. It was Peter who had to change. Peter had to decide whether or not he would become an authentic reconciler. To do that, Paul's confrontation had to touch on Peter's personal walk versus what his misguided peers wanted.

Walking It Out

Living as an authentic reconciler requires taking a firm stance in favor of diversity, privately and publicly. You have to take a personal path over peer pressure. This is exactly what Billy Graham had to do during his 1997 crusade when his privately held value that all people are important to God and, accordingly, must be important to him was challenged.[2] Cognizant of the large Hispanic and Catholic population living in and around the San Antonio region, Graham intentionally held a huge outreach targeting their community. He formed a strategic alliance with Archbishop Patrick Flores, a Mexican-American priest who served as the highest-ranking Catholic clergyman in Texas. Together, they taped radio spots in English and Spanish, encouraging people to attend the crusade to develop a closer relationship with Jesus Christ.

But Billy Graham's commitment to evangelize across cultural lines unnerved some people who did not share the same passion. Some fundamentalists even criticized his cross-cultural approach by posting fliers in downtown San Antonio featuring Graham in a clerical collar with the caption "Reject Billy Graham—He's Too Catholic." Despite the opposition's efforts, the four-day crusade drew a crowd of some 247,500 people. For the first time in its then three-year history, the Alamo dome was filled nightly.

Dr. Graham shared his position on the need to be intentionally cross-cultural when he said in his opening sermon, "The Devil has separated us, and a crusade like this is used of God to bring people of all denominations together.... We need one another."[3] Thousands of Latinos made decisions for Christ. The crusade's success in penetrating the Latino community can be attributed to one man's unwavering commitment to living cross-culturally, even in the face of naysayers. You must do the same. This is what Paul was challenging Peter to do. Peter had to learn how to live above the fear and allure of peer pressure.

3. Practice Advocacy over Silence.

An advocate is a person who defends and pleads in favor of another. The advocate provides public support, recommendation, or argues the needs of the other person be understood and considered. Paul was an advocate for *all the people* in his congregation, even the Gentiles. He could not remain silent and watch the injustice fueling Peter's behavior continue to spread. An authentic reconciler must do the same. That is what Paul was challenging Peter to become. If he was to hold that noble status, Peter had to intentionally practice advocacy over silence. Silence is damning. And silence at the wrong time is sin.

Scripture teaches, "If anyone, then knows the good they ought to do and doesn't do it, it is sin for them" (James 4:17). It's good to love people across the racial divide. It's sin to alienate yourself from them just because they are different from you. Silence is easily misunderstood. That is why Plato said: "I shall assume that your silence gives consent." There is no way Paul could have remained silent. Though Peter was one of the original twelve apostles who walked with Jesus, Paul had to confront his negative behavior. That is what true advocates do. They give voice to the voiceless. Though Peter was one of the foremost Christian leaders at that time in history (as well as in our day through his legacy), Paul had to be emboldened by the Holy Spirit. Right is right and wrong is wrong. Period! Paul called Peter's actions "hypocrisy" because Peter's behavior showed he was concealing his real feelings about Gentiles and diversity. Hypocrisy is not just the concealing of your true feelings; it is masking them under the pretense of better ones.

Paul could not remain silent. He was an advocate for the Gentile members of his flock. Had he remained silent, allowing Peter to save face and return to Jerusalem without any reprimand, the congregation would have felt Paul's silence was also an act of hypocrisy. He did not support Peter's actions. He could not do this and then in the same breath claim to be an advocate. He had to confront him. Silence was not an option. Nobel Peace Prize winner Elie Wiesel said, "I swore never to be silent whenever and wherever human beings endure suffering and humiliation. We must always take sides. Neutrality helps the oppressor, never the victim. Silence encourages the tormentor, never the tormented."[4] Silence legitimizes the victimizer and unintentionally brings more harm to the victims. No wonder Dr. Martin Luther King Jr., said, "In the End, we will remember not the words of our enemies, but the silence of our friends."

To be an advocate in matters of diversity you have to get to know members of the racial group you will be called upon to represent. Advocacy does not mean you totally agree with the values, positions, or views of that group. It simply means you know these people so well, their story, their perspective, and their needs, that you can represent them in an excellent and appropriate way. That was the lesson Peter learned from Paul. Authentic reconcilers must practice advocacy over silence.

Walking It Out

If you've ever watched a National Basketball Association game on television, you know the league is primarily made up of African American players. The complexion of the sport is likely attributable to the huge popularity of basketball in urban communities. In recent years, though, hoop stars are increasingly more diverse, with a large number coming to the NBA from Eastern Europe, Asia, and South America.

Years ago I was invited to serve as a consultant by the Rookies Transition Program, a division within the Players Association of the NBA, to help incoming players become more cross-cultural.

After teaching a session on "How to Connect Across Racial and Cultural Lines" to some eighty NBA rookies, I was immediately pulled into a room by a program coordinator. Through the interpreter, I learned a foreign player felt his game had fallen off because of a huge cultural disconnect between him and his African American teammates. Throughout the season, the African American teammates often teased this international player with playful taunts and trash talk, which is common on urban blacktops all across the country. But their humor was lost on him. He didn't understand why he was being insulted this way. He shut down emotionally and his performance on the basketball court suffered.

I was able to help him see his teammates' words were not intended to be hurtful. I explained that it's common for many within the African American community to tease one another harmlessly. Through his interpreter, I told him African Americans often tease people they like and the teasing he was receiving, though rough at times, reflected their fondness of him. When I said this, his face brightened. I later learned that opening up to me was the first time he'd spoken that entire weekend because of his emotional pain. Identifying the cause of the cultural barrier gave this basketball player a new perspective and insight for building cross-race relationships both on and off the court. I was his advocate to his NBA representatives. They needed to understand how he felt. Advocates represent others when they are unable to represent themselves.

Sociologists Larry Samovar and Richard Porter tell us, "anyone who has truly struggled to comprehend another person—even those closest and most like himself—will appreciate the immensity of the challenge of intercultural communication."[5] In the case of the ball player, five minutes out of my life made a huge difference for his basketball career and his ability to understand others. Authentic reconcilers must not and cannot remain silent. Too much is at stake.

4. Model Diversity Permanently versus Temporarily.

Paul had a fundamental problem with Peter's behavior. The fact that Peter's behavior became monocultural when the Jewish guys came from Jerusalem to Antioch was indicative that his commitment to diversity was short-term and steeped in convenience. It wasn't permanent. This modeled a lukewarm view of diversity. Peter wasn't sold on it as a lifestyle commitment. He was just feigning it while at Antioch. Diversity was outside of his real comfort zone.

Racial reconciliation is a biblical requirement. You have been called to live a multicultural life—permanently. Like Peter, you cannot jump in and out of a multicultural lifestyle. It demands total commitment and not a temporary sacrifice.

Walking It Out

Vacillating back and forth regarding your commitment to diversity is a reflection of a credibility problem. That is what Peter's behavior demonstrated. At its lowest common denominator, credibility reflects honesty of the deepest kind, an honesty that stems from the heart. Without credibility, your relationships can't be healthy. Without credibility, you can't develop cross-cultural relationships.

No matter who you are, you are not exempt from being called on the carpet when your credibility comes into question.

Cross-race relationships are tested in the crucible of life. To deem them strong or healthy they must overcome the nasty pull of prejudice and racial hate that threatens their very existence. Picture two little girls, best of friends, sitting side by side with their backs to the camera, as they dreamily stare at an empty football field. One girl black, the other white. That was the picture of a recent post Rachel Macy Stafford, a *New York Times* bestselling author, put on her Facebook page. Beneath the picture were these words:

> I'll never forget what my daughter said after her best friend was subjected to a racist comment on the school bus one afternoon. "I asked her if she was okay," my child said tearfully. "She didn't say anything, so I just scooted closer." Reluctantly, she admitted, "I didn't know what to do Mama, so I just hurt with her."[6]

Even though Rachel's daughter—the white girl—didn't know what to say to heal the damage of the racial slur inflicted on her best friend, she bravely stood by her side. This is where credibility is earned. You demonstrate empathy, commitment to a person's humanity, even if it calls for your tears to fall alongside hers.

In order to be believable as a reconciler, you vote with your feet and your tears. You stick by your cross-race friend and if need be, you hurt with that friend. This type of action secures your position as an authentic reconciler. Our country, more than ever, needs people like this. Their credibility looms high above the superficiality some display in matters of diversity. Authentic reconcilers hurt alongside of their cross-race friends even if it's not in vogue or commonplace. This demonstrates that a position of pro-diversity is not accidental or temporary, but purposeful and permanent.

Answering the Call to Live Authentically

Are you an authentic reconciler? I pray you are because God called every one of His sons and daughters to the ministry of reconciliation (2 Corinthians 5:18–19). We have an obligation to reconcile people to God, first and foremost, and afterward we must reconcile them to one another. Authentic reconcilers have chosen to honor Jesus' call to obey the whole counsel of the Word of God. There is no other way.

CHAPTER EIGHT

Building a Cross-Cultural Ministry

I opened the book by telling you about my supermarket experience with God and what He asked me as I observed the diverse crowd of shoppers: "David, why can't it be like this in my house?" The question came on the heels of my observation of a diverse crowd of shoppers at the other end of the aisle. Having received God's mandate to build a cross-cultural ministry, I have spent the last thirty-plus years trying to understand the building blocks of this rare ministry model.

Though it shouldn't be rare because diversity is a part of the DNA of a Christian, the multiethnic church remains an anomaly—even in today's supposedly socially progressive generation. Fueled by God's calling on my life and a passion to see the Christian Church equipped with effective cross-cultural ministry tools for the generations to come, I am doggedly committed to changing this paradigm and I trust you will join me.

One observation I've made is that multiracial groupings of people form only when they have a clear benefit. Essentially, the age-old marketing question is raised: What's in it for me? Let's examine this question, ignoring for a moment the self-seeking intent it points out, to see its value in building a cross-cultural ministry.

To better understand, let's look at some secular examples that illustrate the truth. A trip to the local branch of the Department of Motor Vehicles (DMV) will always have a multiracial crowd. Even in rural communities, local citizens know the DMV provides an easy answer to their question of what's in it for me. Whether you need new tags, a replacement driver's license, or a vehicle registration card, the DMV has it. Similarly, the next time you take a trip to the supermarket, do some people watching. You'll likely find people of every stripe, color, and creed shopping. The common need for groceries answers the shopper's fundamental question, "What's in it for me?" But when it comes to the formation of multiracial groups, a deeper observation is needed to determine the common denominator for their formation.

Multiracial groups form because of what the individuals gain from the place where the gathering occurs. Granted, if there are a limited number of supermarkets in your region, people may feel forced to go to the one closest to where they live, rather than driving fifty miles to another city. If we poll people, we'll probably discover a sizable percentage of people make a little longer drive to go to the grocery store where they feel most comfortable shopping, even if it's across town. The same thing occurs with local churches. People will make a longer drive to go where the "what's in it for me" benefit is regularly experienced.

If the local church is to grow in a multiethnic way, it must see the "what's in it for me" question has a spiritual side to it. The question is not carnal or self-absorbed. The question shows you must provide clear benefits if you're to have access to people. They must be able to readily discover a personal gain if they are going to be all in, or at a minimum consider your church as a possible home for their family to worship.

There is a technical term for this sociological reality. It's not simply a business ploy designed to lure more shoppers into a store. The principle is called the *social exchange theory*. The theory says in order for someone of another culture or race to enter the social world of someone of a different culture, that person must *gain* something from that culture that can't be *gained* from his or her own. It was this very theory that became the tool I used to better understand the underpinnings of the multiracial church, which, by definition, is a church with at least 10 percent of its membership falling into a different racial category than the greater population of its members.

My doctoral dissertation focused on diversity in the church.[1] More particularly, I sought to answer the question: What are the essential building blocks of a healthy multiracial and multiethnic congregation? What were the members gaining by being there?

I investigated eight multiracial churches. Each church, at that point in time, had at least 20 percent of its members who were from a different race than the majority. Four churches had black senior pastors and the other four had white senior pastors. Had I included other races of senior pastors to the mix it would have prolonged my research, so I limited my research to the groups with the greatest historic tension and divisions in America. My thought was that if blacks and whites could form healthy cross-race friendships with one another and participate together in the same worship community, the principles would certainly be transferrable to other racial groups.

There was one common thread among the eight churches I investigated. All the folks who connected for over a year at their ministry claimed they gained something unique from the church—something they never gained from a church consisting largely of their own ethnicity.

According to the research data, there are three primary experiences people gain from belonging to a racially and culturally diverse congregation. These three experiences prove to be the building blocks to cross-cultural ministry. I didn't set out with the assumption that since I was pastoring a multiracial congregation, I knew how they are formed. I had some idea, but I wanted answers proven by research and the social science of investigation. When I went into a church with a black senior pastor, I met with a cross-section of white members. I held two ninety-minute focus groups per church. Likewise, in a church with a white senior pastor, I met with African American members who held a wide range of tenure. I also conducted two focus groups with each of those churches.

The Building Blocks

In order to get a fresh perspective of the underpinnings of the multiethnic church, I had to understand what the building blocks were to its appeal across the races. I know I could easily assign the reason for their existence to the *sovereignty of God*. The term *sovereignty* can best be understood when we look to instances recorded in the Bible where God made a decision and then carried it out independent of humanity. These actions, such as creation, point to the fact all things belong to God, such as the Earth, sky, moon, the heavens, silver, gold, and certainly Christians themselves. When God acts sovereignly His people have no right or authority to negotiate, resist, or to partially execute His righteous and just orders. As the King of kings, God can act with divine, uncontested authority in bringing about something that pleases Him.

The 1906 Azusa Street revival in California is an example of a sovereign act of God in modern history that produced a multiracial audience. It happened in 1906 during America's struggle with segregation, overt prejudice, and other social ills that brought about the isolation of the races. For a moment in our history a multiracial gathering occurred in Azusa Street. The famed Pentecostal historian Vinson Synan referenced an eyewitness's account of the revival: "One thing that somewhat surprised me was the presence of so many from different churches. Some were pastors, evangelists, or foreign missionaries. Persons of many nationalities were present."[2] This was a sovereign move of God. We can't replicate it. Plus, this gathering of believers was not drawn together by a church. They were simply hungry for God.

Taking a sovereignty approach would have deprived me of learning about what sparks the formation of the multiracial church. One of my questions to each focus group was, what attracted you to this church and what keeps you here?

The answer always fell into one of three buckets. Each bucket proved to be a building block forming the multiracial church. After reviewing the findings of the two focus groups, along with reviewing the survey data from each church, it was remarkable to find only one of the three building blocks for why that particular congregation formed and maintained its cultural diversity emerged each time. It was never all three. And no two ingredients ever ranked evenly as *the* reason. One always stood out more than the other two. The three building blocks were: 1) the pastor; 2) the worship experience; and, 3) the sense of community.

1. The Pastor

In some multiracial congregations, the pastor was the reason for the formation of those churches and their maintenance. Something unique flowed out of his life and pulpit ministry that attracted people from other races. This was what they *gained* from being connected to that ministry. "The magnanimous character of the pastor keeps me coming back," is what some responders said. Others commented on the pastor's vulnerability and integrity as the basis for their continued engagement. Although the pastor taught them the Bible, people seldom commented on his teaching gift as the reason they stayed.

Their description of what they gained was wholly subjective. Their reasons were based on how they felt being with him. Certainly, the way he presented the Word was cross-cultural. The style of presentation gave every culture equal access to its content. But it was more about *how* they felt *during and after* he shared the Word. Do you remember the way the two disciples felt as they walked together with Jesus on the Road to Emmaus? Jesus was hidden to them the entire journey. They did not know it was Him. When they arrived at their destination, however, their eyes were opened to who He really was. They asked each other, "Were not our hearts burning within us while he talked with us on the road and opened the Scriptures to us?" (Luke 24:33) Although this description of their feelings is subjective to their experience, we understand how they felt.

I'm not equating the pastors to Jesus. I'm equating the experience of how the two disciples described their feelings when Jesus taught them the Word. Notice we did not have a picture of how they felt until they spoke with one another. After voicing their feelings, they realized they shared the same feeling. Similarly, members of my focus groups had no idea other members shared their identical feelings until I held those focus groups and all our eyes were opened.

Some racially diverse congregations form simply because of the pastor. Remove him and a large measure of their diversity will also leave. He is the *gain* people of other races experience whenever they gather.

Getting There

What happens if you're not a pastor? Or, better yet, what happens if you, as a Christian leader, don't have that special something the French call *je ne sais quoi* (pronounced: zhuh nuh se kwa)? Do you throw in the towel concluding you don't have what it takes? No! Don't draw that conclusion, even if you're not a pastor or church leader.

In fact, don't focus on the title "pastor." Focus rather on the primary function of a pastor. Pastors are shepherds. We provide care to people. You do that also and the bigger your heart, the more God will place you in a caring capacity. Your compassion cannot be bottled. It must be expressed toward others. You don't need the title of *pastor* to care. Just care for others wherever you are and in whatever you do vocationally. Care!

There are some Christian leaders who lack a big heart for diversity. Peter was one of them. He was a pastor, yet he failed to demonstrate any special concern or interest in attracting and engaging people from across the cultural divide. Everything shifted, however, after he had an encounter with God. In fact, Peter described his new outlook on life and on people this way: "The truth I have now come to realize," he said, "is that God does not have favorites, but that anybody of any nationality who fears God and does what is right is acceptable to him" (Acts 10:34–35, Jerusalem Bible). If Peter could change, so can you. If Peter could grow in his perspective and attractiveness toward people of other cultures, so can you.

The heart is the starting point. Begin to pray and seek God for a fresh revelation in this area. My friend, Bill Hybels, uses the phrase, "a second conversion" to describe the new outlook he adopted years ago regarding diversity and the church. Bill pastors Willow Creek Community Church in the Chicagoland area. This huge congregation used to be predominantly white. But after Bill's second conversion, the church began to shift its racial and ethnic composition to look more like society.

We all can have a second conversion. It begins in the heart. It begins with you coming face-to-face with God's heart for people. I encourage you to make a special effort to pray and fast for a fresh touch from God in this area of Christian living. In his classic book *The Pursuit of God*, A. W. Tozer wrote, "Come near to the holy men and women of the past and you will soon feel the heat of their desire after God. They mourned for Him, they prayed and wrestled and sought for Him day and night, in season and out, and when they had found Him the finding was all the sweeter for the long seeking."[3] What would happen if you decided to take this year and perhaps next year to pursue the Lord about diversity? I believe the outcome would be "all the sweeter," as Tozer says.

2. The Worship Experience

The second building block I discovered to establishing a multiracial ministry was the worship experience. That was the answer I unearthed when this question was posed to the focus groups: What attracted you and keeps you in this church? In some of the multiracial congregations, the reason for their diversity was not the pastor or the experience of community, it was clearly one other dynamic at work—the worship experience.

Worship is about *entering* the presence of God. The psalmist tells us when we worship we "*enter* his gates with thanksgiving and his courts with praise; give thanks to him and praise his name. For the Lord is good and his love endures forever, his faithfulness continues through all generations" (Psalm 100:4–5, italics mine). There is a twofold focus in public worship. We must focus on God—our primary aim—and we must not overlook our secondary focus—the people. If it's a private time of worship, the focus is a singular one—God is the only one we must engage.

Cross-cultural ministry is being mindful of God *and* the different kinds of people in the room who also came to enter the King's courts and to give Him praise. The moment the leadership, worship team, and the congregation forget this reality, they will lose sight of what keeps the multiracial gathering coming together regularly. Cross-cultural worship is a learned skill and an acquired taste. In every one of the congregations I studied, the subject of cross-cultural worship became part of our discussion without any prompting on my part. People admitted it was an enormous struggle during the early days of their introduction to that ministry. They had to get used to the different genres and styles of music being played and sung, but they hung around and something special began to occur in their hearts. They sensed and experienced unique encounters with the Lord.

Every one of these churches had varying levels of musicianship. Some had professional people at their instruments while others had only amateur musicians. The allure was the love felt when they played and worshiped. It was a love for God and a love for people, all kinds of people. The congregation also played a key role in this. They entered the worship experience without any reservation. They were responsive to the worship team and to entertaining the presence of God. This can be learned. It is not merely the worship team who creates a cross-cultural worship experience. The congregation—the sum of the individuals present—also produces the experience. The congregation encourages the worship team to continue creating those kinds of experiences by its responsiveness.

Getting There

My wife, Marlinda, is the worship pastor at Christ Church. Over three decades of ministry we've become quite adept at creating weekly cross-cultural worship experiences for the congregation. But it wasn't always that way. Many of the people who joined the church and the worship team came from musical backgrounds that were largely monocultural. Broadening their musical palate took some work and creativity. It wasn't just about singing songs from across different genres, it was about doing it authentically and from a servant's heart. Authenticity is conveying genuineness and realism in an unforced manner. Our people found joy in singing music they *wanted* to sing not music they *had* to sing. This perspective goes back to my comments in a previous chapter about tolerance versus accommodation. We all want to be accommodated, planned for in advance, and not tolerated—even when it comes to the music we sing.

Again, this is a heart thing. You can't fake or be "educated" into it. Although your mind plays an integral role, the mind can only submit when the heart has first surrendered to the value of loving people across the racial divide. To really develop and convey this sense of authenticity, which is essential in creating cross-cultural worship experiences, authenticity is undergirded by service. Marlinda teaches our worship leaders they are servants. They are first servants of God and then servants of God's people—His multicolored people.

Paul described the attitude and the order of priority of a servant of God when he said to the Galatians, "Am I now trying to win the approval of human beings, or of God? Or am I trying to please people? If I were still trying to please people, I would not be a servant of Christ" (Galatians 1:10). But he didn't stop there, he went on to say in the same letter to the same people, "You, my brothers and sisters, were called to be free. But do not use your freedom to indulge the flesh; rather, *serve one another* humbly in love" (Galatians 5:13, italics mine). A principal qualification of being a worship leader, the one charged with carrying out the church's missional heart toward diversity in music, is having a servant's heart.

A servant seeks to execute the will, desires, and interests of the master in a pleasant manner. Good servants study the moods of their masters, learning what to say when, and even what to present to them at a given moment. Good worship is about knowing God's moods and singing songs that will entertain His presence at a particular time. Marlinda puts our multiple worship teams on reading programs. They must become good students of God. Knowing God is a huge part of worship.

The flip side is equally true; knowing about people, their tendencies, moods, and how to engage their hearts around spiritual things is extremely important. To serve a multiracial group of people, you must learn about their cultures, history, and even some of the injustices they have experienced. A focused reading program helps accomplish this aspect of training others to serve. This newfound knowledge will equip the worship team to know how to create an atmosphere and a song list that enables various ethnic groups to say like the psalmist, "Help, God—the bottom has fallen out of my life! Master, hear my cry for help! Listen hard! Open your ears! Listen to my cries for mercy" (Psalm 130:1, The Message). The idea here is, if you really care about others in worship, your care for them will help create such an atmosphere that lets them unburden their souls in the presence of God. Isn't that a large aspect of biblical worship?

To really help our worship teams develop a servant's heart toward the congregation, Marlinda encourages them to participate in humanitarian efforts like volunteering with Habitat for Humanity. This organization builds homes for under-resourced people. Can you imagine a group of worship leaders volunteering at Habitat? It sounds odd, doesn't it? If someone asks them, why are *you* volunteering, they'll most likely respond: "I want to help build a home for a needy family, and I want to become a better worship leader." The first part we all get, but the second part of their answer requires a bit more probing. We discovered that service in one area has transferable benefits in another, completely unrelated area.

The worship experience was what many in some of the multi-racial churches claimed was their "gain." They remained in the church largely because their souls had been nourished and well-fed by the weekly encounters they had during the worship times.

3. The Sense of Community

A third building block unearthed during the focus group study was "the sense of community" people experienced in the forming and maintaining of their racially diverse congregations. One African American lady commented, "I feel at home here." Without any hesitation, she blurted out those words in response to my question, "What attracted you to the church and keeps you here?" That was her answer as well as the answer for dozens of others.

When I tallied the responses from the focus groups, there was no close second regarding what kept them there. People felt like they belonged. They felt welcomed. There was a high degree of friendship that kept the congregations of these multiracial churches united.

No one claimed it was "the pastor" or "the worship experience" that kept them there. I'm not suggesting people didn't love their pastors or enjoy their church's worship experience. The stark reality was the "gain" for the minority population in some of the multiracial congregations was simply the sense of community they experienced. It wasn't forced or manufactured. People felt a genuine sense of belonging. They felt like insiders and members of the team. Some said, "I feel like this is my family."

Getting There

I've learned some things don't come naturally to people. They must be intentionally worked on. If your church is not the friendliest group of people, particularly toward outsiders, it's important you do something about it. Perhaps you can suggest the idea of forming a small group program to the leaders. This is a great way to help people forge knitted relationships. And, even if your church is not inclined to go that route, ask if you can form a single small group that focuses on diversity.

Small groups increase people's satisfaction with their church. This statement is not just my opinion; it was proven during my research of the eight multiracial churches. In fact, the churches with small groups were the ones who voiced the sense of community as their "gain" and were the congregations scoring highest in membership satisfaction.

Small groups provide an opportunity for you to make friends. This private, more intimate, experience brings you into someone's life at a faster pace than seeing him or her weekly at worship. There's no doubt a strong correlation exists between the increased opportunities to form healthy cross-race friendships when small groups are present at a church. Yet, we are without excuse because small groups are only meaningful if those who participate have a heart for people. The heart for people is what creates the sense of community. Small groups are just the vehicle through which a sense of community can easily operate. You don't need a small group to show that kind of care, though. It can happen anywhere, if you truly care.

The story below illustrates how our own personal commitment to developing cross-race relationships can provide personal gain. A graduate student was required to live with a Navajo family for several months to complete his dissertation on the Navajo Indians. The matriarch of the family, a wise old grandmother, spoke no English and the doctoral student spoke no Navajo. Yet a bond developed between the two, partly with the help of the old woman's children, who spoke English. The student and the grandmother grew very close.

Several months later, when the graduate student completed his research, it was time for him to return to the university. The members of the Navajo village threw a farewell party for him. After the party, he was getting into his car when he saw the grandmother walking out of the house with tears streaming down her cheeks. She came right up to the student, the first white friend she'd had in her eighty-two years of life. She tenderly placed one hand on the left side of his face and the other hand softly on his right cheek, looked him square in the eyes and said in the best English she could muster, "I like me best when I'm with you."

At that, the young man lost it. He and the grandmother wept together because they personally experienced how crossing cultures brings out the best in you. When we remain in our own cultural world, parts of us—the good parts, the lovely parts, and the culturally important parts—lie dormant. Consider implementing one or all three building blocks in your life and ministry this year. A good place to begin is by launching a reading group focused on the topic of diversity. See where it goes. My prayer for you is you will one day be able to look someone of another race in the eyes and say, "I like me best when I'm with you."

The Future of the Church

Admittedly, we don't know all there is to know about the multiracial church. More research and investigation is needed. Because of the browning of America, we must encourage researchers, sociologists, and theologians to feed us this sorely needed information—and the need is only going to grow. If we don't gain a greater understanding behind the formation and maintenance of these kinds of churches, the Church will either repel potential members or make it hard from them to join its ranks. This is clearly not God's plan or design. Let these three building blocks move you and your church in the right direction.

We must always keep in mind we're building the Church not just for ourselves but for coming generations. We must leave a legacy that aligns with Sacred Scripture. If not, our children and their children's children will have to work harder to develop local churches that look and function according to the pattern of the New Testament.

CHAPTER NINE

Leading across Cultures

Have you ever heard of a white leader addressing a crowd of angry African Americans on the heels of a racially motivated crime when the audience was respectful and courteous toward him? I have. In this leader's community, a recent accidental shooting of an African American youth by a white police officer had everyone up in arms. The community was a social tinderbox. As this white leader stood in front of the hurting crowd, his compassion and grief were palpable. His teary eyes expressed his empathy and feelings of loss over such a young life cut short. His role as a pastor, someone trained to understand how to connect with grieving people, added to his social stature.

This particular white leader had influence across cultures. I had to find out what made him so special. During my personal interview with this pastor, he said something quite memorable: "I have earned the right to influence African Americans and to be listened to by them." He was on to something. My dissertation research took another turn. I had to learn the answer to this question: "Does a pastor's view on race relations have any influence on his congregation?" In short, the answer is yes.

A pastor can have influence across the range of cultures both inside and outside his church, but there are some prerequisites he must meet. Let's take a step back and agree on one simple point: leadership is influence. Leading across cultures is the ability to influence people, their decisions, and the visionary goals of the organization or work group across cultures. Although I will provide some insight on the role of leaders within the church and their impact on the interracial health of the congregation, the principles apply in most other contexts. You may be tasked with leading a school, a department at work, or a community group; apply what you learn here, and watch the health of the cross-race relationships in your midst soar to new heights.

Your personal views on matters of race and culture have the capacity to influence how others feel on that subject. Invariably, when I travel, leaders often pull me to the side and ask: "How do I solve this race problem in my congregation?" Then they lay out for me the problem, which is usually some issue between a black and a white member.

Most of the time a leader knows what to do, but when it comes to race relations, some leaders become immobilized and their leadership is stifled. In my opinion, addressing a race-related problem is a perfect leadership opportunity to influence your community regarding God's perspective on race relations. But for some odd reason, leaders just shut down. The fact of the matter is some leaders are afraid to be labeled as racist, bigoted, or some other negative tag by one of the squabbling members or witnesses. But it doesn't have to be that way if you learn how to navigate these murky waters.

Silence, neutrality, or withdrawal are social tools that should never be in the leader's toolkit. In fact, they hurt people on multiple levels. Most significantly, they indicate your leadership is not practiced in matters of race relations. On the other hand, my research showed when a pastor's values and behavior emphasized positive race relations, a greater cohesiveness in cross-race relationships was produced in his congregation. The two actions providing the most influence across cultures were his *accepting diversity* and his *modeling diversity* publicly. When these two elements were present, his leadership had influence across cultures. Conversely, when he was silent on the issue and kept his view of diversity strictly personal, he had no authority to intervene or lead across cultural lines.

These two actions can be integrated into everyone's social skill set. You need not be a pastor to have influence. You just need to see yourself as someone whom others look to, or can look to in matters of care, empathy, guidance, and plain old wisdom. If you lead a Girl Scout troop, a community garden club, or a department at work, your positive values and behavior toward cross-race relationships will have a huge influence on the people in your midst. It's not your title that gives you influence over others, it's your willingness to let God use you where He has planted you.

The reason the white pastor I referenced at the top of this chapter had influence over the African Americans within his community during this time of racial unrest was because they knew where he stood on race relations. I learned this white pastor marched with Dr. Martin Luther King Jr., during the civil rights movement. His accepting and modeling diversity during that and other fragile moments earned him the right to influence across cultures. You can earn that same right, but you cannot remain silent on your views. People must know where you stand ahead of time if you're going to have the ability to influence others across cultures.

Earning the Right to Influence

When the church at Antioch was formed, might I say in an unintentional way, the multiethnic congregation knew they needed a pastor—a leader who would help them grow in their relationship with the Lord. Most new church plants start with a pastor and then a congregation forms around him or her. The Antioch Church formed because zealous believers shared their faith with irreligious people. They then went on a search for a pastor who would lead them.

The only established church at that point in history was the church at Jerusalem, which was a monocultural church. Its members' experience interacting with other cultures around spiritual issues was limited to none. When news of the move of God (Acts 11:21) came to their attention, however, they quickly sent Barnabas to Antioch. Scripture says, "He was a good man, full of the Holy Spirit and faith, and a great number of people were brought to the Lord" (Acts 11:24).

Why Barnabas? Why not some other, more experienced leader? Why didn't they send one of the original apostles—someone who had firsthand experience being with Jesus? Certainly one of those men knew the gospel message and could easily teach it. Why were none of them handed this exciting ministry assignment? The reason was a singular one. Barnabas was a cross-cultural leader and they were not. Barnabas' extensive experience in diverse circles was unearthed because of the city in which he was raised. He was from Cyprus (Acts 4:36), which was a mecca for racial, cultural, and ethnic diversity. Apart from his ability to teach Scripture and lead, he was a cross-cultural leader. "Send him," was the popular vote of the leaders of the Jerusalem Church.

It's one thing for you to be cross-cultural on a personal level, but a completely different thing for you to exercise good leadership across cultures. In the same way, you can be an excellent musician, but that doesn't mean you'll make for an excellent orchestra conductor. The latter requires the ability, patience, and willingness to bring an entire ensemble of various instruments together so their collective sound is melodious and entertaining. You may be an excellent ball player, but that doesn't automatically ensure you'll be a good coach. A coach must know how to work with the various skill levels of his players and position them in the right spots for the benefit of the team while working with a full array of personalities. I can draw the same conclusion across every discipline.

To effectively influence across cultures, four intentional actions must be taken by a cross-cultural leader. He or she must be able to:

1. Liberate the people.
2. Listen to the people.
3. Lead the people.
4. Love the people.

When these four actions are employed, rest assured you will have remarkable influence across all cultures. Good leadership is never resisted, at least not for long. Everyone celebrates when his team wins. No one likes being on a losing team.

1. Liberate the People.

Since leadership is influence, effective leaders spend quite a bit of time locating the people. Where are they emotionally? Where are they in their commitment to the group? And certainly where are they in their view of the gospel presentation? Two behavioral scientists, Laura Paglis and Stephen Greene, defined leadership this way: "Leadership is the process of diagnosing where the work group is now and where it needs to be in the future, and formulating a strategy for getting there. Leadership also involves implementing change through developing a base of influence with followers, motivating them to commit to and work hard in pursuit of change goals, and working with them to overcome obstacles to change."[1]

You cannot lead a multicultural group or department if you have no idea where its members are in their view of things. Successful leaders observe and listen. They are looking for clues, key information that will aid them in providing answers that will guide their diverse constituency toward the organizational goals. In a church context, we cannot lead a diverse team if we have not discovered its take on how Jesus is being presented to them. Are their souls being fed? Do they regularly encounter God in worship? These questions are critical for locating where a person is in his or her satisfaction with the church and with the Lord. And finding the answers boils down to how you present your views regarding the doctrine of salvation.

The leader's job is to liberate the people from all sorts of bondage. At the launch of Jesus' ministry He announced, "The Spirit of the Lord is on me, because he has anointed me to preach good news to the poor. He [God] has sent me to proclaim freedom for the prisoners and recovery of sight for the blind, to release the oppressed, to proclaim the year of the Lord's favor" (Luke 4:18-19). Notice, Jesus told us His entire ministry is about liberation and if that is the intent of our Master's focus, we must follow suit in a multicultural context.

Present the Biblical Meaning of Salvation

In his book *Out of Every Tribe and Nation*, famed theologian Justo González asked, "What do we mean by salvation?" The meaning of salvation becomes more real to the individual within a multiethnic setting when the word is tied to terms such as *salvation*, *struggle*, and *survival*. Salvation then "means both the individual daily survival and our survival as a people or a culture."[2] People have to see and understand the global definition of salvation. Every culture must gain equal access to the Cross and the power of the Resurrection. Without that, they will slowly drift away from your church to seek fellowship in a place where their needs are better understood and addressed.

In the early days of my ministry there was a single parent who began attending our weekend services. She came to know our church through a street evangelization project. She had five children by multiple fathers. I noticed after a few weeks she'd stopped coming. Since the church was under one hundred members at that time, I was the follow-up department. After tracking her down, I learned of the reason. She said, "You guys speak about marriage and family a lot. I see only married couples and single people at your church who don't have children. At best, they have one child. My family structure doesn't fit. I realize my mistakes, but where do I go to receive instruction and feel a sense of belonging despite my broken past?"

Her answer brought a fuller perspective to how I would approach the subject of family going forward. It impacted the way I would represent God and His love in our broken, fragmented culture. People want to see themselves in how we unpack the Scriptures and major themes such as the meaning of salvation. If they don't, they will check out.

To further bolster his argument of the need of the multiethnic church to have a holistic approach to salvation and ministry, Justo González quotes the Japanese American theologian Lloyd K. Wake. Wake says, "For Asian-Americans, salvation goes beyond a theological doctrine, or a metaphysical concept. It relates to rice and tea issues of survival—identity, self-worth, personal and community dignity, self-determination, justice and physical existence in a physical space. It is the well-being not only of the soul and spirit, but of the body."[3] In essence, marginalized groups in the broader society cannot have that same experience in the Church, especially a multiethnic church. If they do, they will see no difference between our broken society and the Church.

Cross-Cultural Coaching

I used to assist the chaplain's office for the New York Giants and Jets whenever they called upon me. I'd teach Bible studies and engage interested players in spiritual conversations. Sometimes these studies would take place at players' homes. This up-close interaction also gave me an opportunity to meet some of the coaches. Apart from the head coach, the typical NFL team has fifteen other highly skilled assistant coaches to help the players reach their potential. Imagine that. These coaches are charged with the responsibility to help each player liberate and unlock his potential as a professional athlete. Coaching brings out the best in you.

Have you ever considered getting a cross-cultural coach? I mean having someone, or a team of people, in your life for a short stint, say six months, to help you improve your ability to connect with people across cultural lines. I have done that over the years to improve my preaching skills. I exposed myself to the process of accepting constructive feedback from various cross-cultural experts, particularly to answer the question: How does my preaching come across within the Asian community, the Latino world, or even white America? I recognized I couldn't get this information by drawing my own conclusion or based on my own gut reaction. That's flawed data. In the same way, I can't give you an accurate answer to the question: How am I doing as a husband? You'd have to ask my wife. Likewise, to the question: How am I doing as a dad? You'd have to ask my two daughters. And if you're like me, you'll have to poll someone from one of the racial groups in your sphere to assess your effectiveness as a cross-cultural communicator.

The point I'm making is that in some matters, especially regarding matters of the heart, you need others to critique and guide you toward reaching greater levels of effectiveness. The only way to really know how to impact constituents of certain racial and cultural groups, especially when it comes to liberation, is to learn from them how well you're doing. Their answers will help you discover what you need to do to grow. For example, Puerto Rican theologian Miguel A. De La Torre writes, "For a large number of Euroamericans, Hispanics are (a) lazy, unproductive, unenterprising—the sleeping Mexican with the wide sombrero, drinking tequila and whiling away the day against a wall, or a bunch of open-shirted Caribbean men drinking beer and playing dominoes at a local, run-down park."[4] When a Hispanic has to work through those negative images on a daily basis, whether at work or in the community, it wears on him. So, the Church must become a place of refuge, liberation, and image-building, if we are to be his community too. We are our brother's keeper. That means, the responsibility to bind up the wounds of the members of our spiritual family is yours and mine.

In the case of Barnabas and the Antioch Church, after some time he realized he was not the right man to serve as the primary leader of that group, so he personally recruited Paul to take over (Acts 11:25–26). Barnabas didn't leave Antioch, he simply served the church in a different pastoral capacity. He became like one of the assistant NFL coaches supporting the head coach. By admitting the second seat was a better fit for him, Barnabas demonstrated the maturity of his character. It also showed he cared so much for the people's liberation and spiritual growth he didn't allow his ego to interrupt their trajectory. Leading across cultures is about identifying the right people to sit in the right seats on the bus. This way the bus (a.k.a. the Church) can move toward the purpose of God.

2. Listen to the People.

Listening is a difficult but learnable skill. It requires patience, focus, and certainly the alignment of outcomes. You should want the same outcome as the person to whom you're listening. You both should want a Christ-glorifying solution to the problem or conflict being discussed. When you listen, you demonstrate care, empathy, and the fact the other person has value and worth. This is critical, especially in a multiethnic setting.

In his book, *Black and White Styles in Conflict*, Thomas Kochman, professor of communication and theater at the University of Illinois, writes: "When I meet minority students in my classes for the first time, I know that where I stand with respect to issues and my personal philosophy will be as important to them as what I know about their language and culture. I also know that I need to indicate where I am going with the information. Consequently, information is presented not just as an interesting set of facts but for the sake of argument. Argument in turn is presented for the sake of persuasion, and persuasion for the sake of social change."[5] Kochman is implying his lectures have much to do with his ability to listen to his ethnically diverse students if he's to influence them. He cannot influence them if they don't feel heard. Listening is a critical component in leadership.

The Bible doesn't come right out and say it, but we can extract from the text that Barnabas was listening to the people. Either they voiced the need for new senior leadership or Barnabas brought it up once he saw his inadequacy. Regardless of the origin, Barnabas was listening to the people—either with his ears or with his heart. The result was amazing. Paul was brought in as the lead pastor and the church continued to experience growth, and growth across cultures (Acts 11:26).

In 2005, I served as a member of the executive committee for the Billy Graham crusade held in New York City—the last one of his life. I took away thousands of lessons about walking in humility, staying focused on the mission of the gospel, and maintaining Christ-centered living amidst pluralism. But one lesson I'll never forget was the unwavering commitment of the Graham organization to include every culture and ethnic group in the planning stages of the crusade. Each month we met, the Asian, African American, Caucasian, Native American, Latino, and Messianic Jewish communities were all represented in the strategy room. If the intent of the crusade was to reach the whole city, a cross-section of the cultures of the city was needed in the planning stages. The Graham organization modeled the importance of listening to qualify itself to lead across cultures.

Listen for Cultural Information

Poor listening skills create conflict. I had to learn that vital lesson if I was to be effective at cross-cultural evangelism. I completed my master's degree in engineering at Stevens Institute of Technology in Hoboken, New Jersey. Back then, there were several Asian students living on campus. I was twenty years old, but only about five months old in my faith. Tony, one of the more mature Christian students at Stevens, took me under his wing, mentoring me in how to share my faith. We'd meet twice a week, and then walk around on campus sharing our faith. Sometimes we'd knock on dorm doors to see which students were interested in striking up a conversation.

One evening we engaged a guy from Vietnam in a spiritual conversation. Let's name him Chi. In about fifteen minutes Chi was praying with me to receive Christ. After we left Chi, Tony expressed disapproval in my haste to pray with this international student. I didn't understand what the problem was until Tony, a fellow African American, spelled it out for me. He said, "You were not listening to Chi! Don't just listen to his words; listen to his culture. Guys from that part of the world don't like to disappoint people. He did not understand what you were sharing with him about Jesus. He wasn't ready to accept Christ as his Savior. He just wanted to please you." Wow! Did I blow it or what? At that point, I had extremely little experience dealing with people from that part of the world. This tidbit of cultural information made a huge difference in my approach to evangelism from that point forward.

Listening is not just about hearing; it's about hearing from a cultural perspective. Some cultures are more aggressive than others. The reverse is equally true. Some cultures are more compliant and easy going than others. One is not better than the other; they're just different. Knowing the difference comes from observing and listening to people. Seek to listen not just with your ears but also with your heart.

Over the years I've become quite fascinated with historic intercessors—men and women who sought God for the transformation of their generation. One admirable man of prayer was John Hyde. Prayer was such a pillar to his ministry he earned the nickname Praying Hyde. While in India, Hyde struggled to master the language. He loved the people and they felt his care for them. Yet his struggle with the language was so tough the missionary organization that sent him there voted for his return to the States. When news of that decision reached the ears of the Indian people they protested, saying: "If he never speaks the language of our lips, he speaks the language of our hearts."[6]

The prayer life of this man of God created such a connection with the people he served they willingly went to the mat for him. That's proof that listening is a major part of leading across cultures. I want to both challenge and encourage you to listen. Listen to the people God sends your way. Listen to their cries. Listen to their laughter. Listen to their hearts!

3. Lead the People.

In the early days of my ministry, I used to regularly complain to my wife that I didn't have the leaders I needed to get the job done. One day, Marlinda reached her limit with my complaining. She said, in a very pleasant yet challenging manner, "Why don't you do something about it rather than complain?"

She hit the ball back into my court, and it forced me to come up with a strategy to develop leaders. Seldom do people come to us ready-made. They need work. They need coaching and mentoring.

Over the years I've established several development programs aimed at helping emerging leaders grow into their potential. From reading plans to case study analyses and focused conversations around various leadership themes, I've used a variety of methods to develop leaders. When it comes to influencing others across racial lines, I've had great successes with some trainees. Yet I've seen others struggle to engage people on a cross-cultural platform. These trainees often held a posture of superiority and heavy-handedness with people. They weren't aware of their behavior and they'd refuse to see themselves even when I attempted to gently show them their short-sightedness. Instead, they'd blame others for not responding positively to their leadership style. This only alienated people and watered down the trainees' influence in our ministry.

There's too much at stake to promote someone to a position where he'll just end up being divisive. And while the person's heart may be in a good place, his style of leadership takes everyone he touches to a place of segmentation and cultural separation. Imagine the apostle Peter, in his monocultural style, being released to do high-level ministry at the church at Antioch. It would have been a train wreck. That beautiful multiethnic congregation would have slowly dissolved into a flawed expression of church. It would have become a monocultural body of believers in short order. To assume a leadership spot in a multiethnic congregation or other organization, your personal style of leadership must unite and not divide the people. It must also awaken a heart in others to grow cross-culturally.

If leadership means influence, you must be able to influence others not only across cultures but to also cause those in your midst to grow cross-culturally in their own lives. Nowadays we're hearing about suicide bombers and other terrorists becoming radicalized through the influence of other haters. Some of these people are being radicalized through the Internet. Others go off to remote camps in countries like Syria and Afghanistan to develop their hatred to new levels. The word *radicalized* means "to make someone become more radical [extreme] in their political or religious beliefs."[7] Imagine that a person's level of hatred can be stoked by someone who holds an even greater disdain for people unlike himself. These intense haters create an atmosphere and a hunger for hate and more hate. Their social cancer is contagious to people who already have a taste for hatred.

What would happen if you turned this societal problem on its head? What would happen if you learned how to stoke someone's cross-cultural appetite in a loving way? We would be able to stomp out prejudice and bigotry, that's what. It wouldn't be able to stand against the power of people sold out to loving their neighbors as themselves. This is what happened at Antioch. These radicalized believers unintentionally launched the Antioch Church—the first multiethnic congregation.

When people were turning to Jesus left and right from across the cultural divide, the Scripture says, "News of this reached the church in Jerusalem, and they sent Barnabas to Antioch. When he arrived and *saw what the grace of God had done*, he was glad and encouraged them all to remain true to the Lord with all their hearts" (Acts 11:22–23, italics mine). God's grace was at work in bridging the culture gap and uniting people around the message of Jesus Christ. I love how Bible teacher James Ryle defines *grace*. He says, "*Grace is the empowering presence of God enabling you to be who God created you to be, and to do what God has called you to do.*"[8]

We must pray God's grace goes into effect in our churches and communities. Without it, it will be humanly impossible to build healthy cross-cultural ministries no matter how effective our leadership is. We need God's help to please God. And, we need God's help to please people, His multicultural people. That's the bottom line.

4. Love the People.

I remember asking a Chinese leader in my neighboring state of New York, "How can I reach the Chinese within my northern

New Jersey community?" His answer was simple yet profound. He said, "Love their children and you'll win them." He unpacked his statement a little further. "Offer programs for kids," he said. "If you can demonstrate to the parents that you love their kids, you'll win the parents over." I've endeavored to integrate his "love strategy" into my evangelistic practices.

The difficulty, at least for me, is my actions of love sometimes are not interpreted as such. They are often interpreted as merely opportunities for family ministry. I'm still working on the messaging of our outreaches so people will sense our love for them. It's like helping your children understand your parental actions are steeped in love. Sometimes they don't see that. They just eat the cereal, shove the chair under the table when finished, and then run off and play. It may take years for them to see that buying their favorite cereal, ensuring there's milk in the fridge, bowls and spoons in the cupboard, and a table and chair to eat on are expressions of your love. Yet, you get up every morning and go through the same parental practices knowing that they are too immature, too disconnected from the finer points of adult reality, to recognize what you've done and will continue doing for them.

If you think about it on a higher level, a more theological one, God's loving actions toward humanity have been gravely misunderstood and viewed as insignificant. Yet, it was His one and only Son who was sacrificed on the cross as a display of His redemptive love for each of us. How many people live their lives without considering the magnitude of this most generous gift to mankind? Our ignorance of God's loving actions doesn't deter Him from remaining faithful. Let's follow His lead and love people across the cultural divide even if our actions are taken for granted.

Love Requires Making Room in Your Heart

To love people, you must make room in your heart for them. Your love for them should not be based on what they do or don't do. Christians are called to love people, even the unlovable ones. Christians are called to love people through actions and not merely with words. This truth is illustrated in a story the theologian William Barclay tells about a group of World War II soldiers. The soldiers lost a friend in battle and wanted to give their fallen comrade a decent burial. They found a church with a graveyard behind it surrounded by a white fence. They asked the parish priest if their friend could be buried in the church's graveyard.

"Was he Catholic?" the priest inquired.

"No, he was not," answered the soldiers.

"I'm sorry, then," said the priest. "Our graveyard is reserved for members of the holy Church. But you can bury your friend outside the fence. I will see that the gravesite is cared for."

"Thank you, Father," said the soldiers, and they proceeded to bury their friend just outside the graveyard, on the other side of the fence.

When the war ended, the soldiers decided to visit the gravesite of their friend before returning home. They remembered the location of the church and the grave, just outside the fence. They searched for it but couldn't find it. Finally, they went to the priest to inquire about its location.

"Sir, we cannot find our friend's grave."

"Well," answered the priest, "after you buried your fallen friend, it just didn't seem right to me that he should be buried outside the fence."

"So, you moved his grave?" asked the soldiers.

"No," said the priest. "I moved the fence."[9]

To love people from across the racial divide, you must be willing to move your fence to include them in your heart.

Conclusion

One of the sobering realities of being a Christian is remembering we're in a war—a spiritual war. Paul said, "Put on the full armor of God, so that you can take your stand against the devil's schemes" (Ephesians 6:11). This war is also a social one involving value systems that clash against one another. On a daily basis we're challenged to live above this world's culture by living in alignment with Scripture. Wary of the culture and race wars, Paul reminds Timothy "no one serving as a soldier gets entangled in civilian affairs, but rather tries to please his commanding officer" (2 Timothy 2:4). This reminder provides two pieces of advice: we're commanded to love and we're commanded to serve as soldiers in God's army.

We're Commanded to Love

First, Jesus is our commanding officer. We serve at His pleasure. He is our boss. We use the weapons He gives us and His weapon of love is most powerful. It can conquer the hardest of hearts. We win people by loving them into the kingdom of God. Afterward, we teach them how to love *their* neighbors as themselves. We've been commanded to love even across cultures. Sometimes doing this can be very trying. Because we're His soldiers, ordered to love our neighbors as we love ourselves, we do our best to please our commanding officer.

An elderly South African woman stood in an emotionally charged courtroom listening to white police officers acknowledging the atrocities they perpetrated in the name of apartheid. During these court proceedings, a man named Officer Van der Broek acknowledged his responsibility in the death of her son. Van der Broek, along with others, shot her eighteen-year-old son at point-blank range. He and the others partied while they burned his body, turning it over on the fire until it was ashes.

Eight years later, Van der Broek and others arrived to seize her husband. To make matters worse, Van der Broek came to fetch the woman hours later, taking her to a woodpile where her husband lay bound. She was forced to watch as they poured gasoline over his body and ignited the flames that consumed his body. The last words her husband said were, "Forgive them."

Now, Van der Broek stood awaiting judgment. South Africa's Truth and Reconciliation Commission asked the woman what she wanted. "Three things," she said. "I want Mr. Van der Broek to take me to the place where they burned my husband's body. I would like to gather up the dust and give him a decent burial. Second, Mr.

Van der Broek took all my family away from me, and I still have a lot of love to give. Twice a month, I would like for him to come to the ghetto and spend a day with me so I can be a mother to him. Third, I would like Mr. Van der Broek to know that he is forgiven by God and that I forgive him too. I would like someone to lead me to where he is seated so I can embrace him and he can know my forgiveness is real."

As the elderly woman was led across the courtroom, Van der Broek fainted. Someone began singing "Amazing Grace." Gradually everyone joined in.[1]

This elderly woman was a soldier of Christ Jesus. Her expression of love toward her former oppressor, though bighearted and gracious, was really just a reflection of this one thing: she was doing what she had been ordered to do. She was pleasing her commanding officer by loving across cultural lines. She was loving Mr. Van der Broek.

We're Commanded to Serve

Timothy was a soldier of Jesus Christ, as are we. In that capacity we must always be vigilant in fighting the good fight of faith. Good soldiers must maintain their fighting shape. We must never let wounds, pain, trials, and other difficulties dull our warrior instincts. If we do, we become casualties. Wounded soldiers can't give themselves to fighting against the culture wars. We cannot allow ourselves to remain wounded by prejudice. It would render us unloving, because we'd prove to be prejudiced too. We must be able to love across cultures. We're soldiers of love.

Our duty to the Lord is for eternity. We can never return to civilian life. Paul was reminding Timothy he could not succumb to hate or neutrality. He was a soldier on a lifelong mission of love. Christians must abide by the same mantra our Marines adopted years ago: "Once a Marine, always a Marine."

In 1941 during World War II (1939–1945), Japanese soldier Hiroo Onoda was sent to a small U.S. occupied island in the Philippines. His orders were to hamper enemy attacks and spy on U.S. forces on the island. He joined forces with a group of soldiers already stationed there. However, within a month, all the men were killed in battle, with the exception of four of them. Hiroo and the others took to the hills.

In 1945, four years later, they began seeing pamphlets stating the war had ended. Given the psychological nature of war, Onoda dismissed the news as propaganda. Over the next few years the other soldiers surrendered or died, one by one. But Onoda held his position, even continuing his guerilla activities until 1974, some twenty-nine years later.

Onoda finally met a college dropout named Suzuki who was backpacking in the island and explained to him the war had ended. Still, the dedicated soldier was reluctant to believe the war was over. He did not until his former commanding officer, then retired for many years, flew to the island and gave Onoda a final order. Lay down your arms is what he said, and in obedience Lieutenant Onoda did.[2]

You must follow suit in today's race wars. You must keep loving people, crossing cultural lines, and building healthy cross-race friendships even when some may fail. The only time you have the right to quit is when your commanding officer—the Lord Jesus Christ—tells you to lay down your arms. Until then, man your post. You've been commanded to serve in the King's army.

Notes

Introduction
1.   "Choice Quotes," SermonIllustrations.com, http://www.sermonillustrations.com/a-z/c/choice.htm.

Chapter 1
1.   "A John 3:16 Love Story," Trusting in the Word, http://www.trustingintheword.net/John316.htm.
2.   William Douglas Chamberlain, *The Meaning of Repentance*, (Philadelphia, PA: Westminster Press, 1943), 23.
3.   "Mark Twain Quotes," Goodreads.com, http://www.goodreads.com/quotes/404897-keep-away-from-people-who-try-to-belittle-your-ambitions.
4.   "Ralph Waldo Emerson Quotes," Goodreads.com, http://www.goodreads.com/quotes/74783-what-i-need-is-someone-who-will-make-me-do.
5.   Milton Rokeach, *Beliefs, Attitudes, and Values: A Theory of Organization and Change* (San Francisco: Jossey-Bass, 1968).
6.   "Off the Grid: Why Americans Don't Travel Abroad," Paste, April 14, 2016. https://www.pastemagazine.com/articles/2016/04/off-the-grid-why-americans-travel-domestic-instead-1.html .
7.   Reena Ninan, "Father Bares Some Skin in Daisy Dukes to Teach Daughter a Lesson," ABC News, September 13, 2013, https://gma.yahoo.com/blogs/abc-blogs/father-bares-skin -daisy-dukes-teach-daughter-lesson-130620319--abc-news -parenting.html (accessed April 21, 2015).
8.   "Why Starbucks' Race Together Campaign Failed," Eater Starbucks, June 18, 201,https://www.eater.com/2015/6/18/8807849/why-starbucks-race-together-campaign-failed.

Chapter 2

1. H. Richard Niebuhr, *Christ and Culture* (New York: Harper & Row, 1951), 33.
2. Charles H. Dodd, *Dynamics of Intercultural Communication* (New York: McGraw-Hill, 1998), 275.
3. Reinhold Niebuhr, "The Serenity Prayer."
4. William B. Gudykunst and Young Yun Kim, *Communicating with Strangers: An Approach to Intercultural Communication* (New York: McGraw-Hill, 1997), 17.
5. "Dr. Martin Luther King's Quote," GodandCulture.com, http://www.godandculture.com/blog/sunday-at-11-the-most-segregated-hour-in-this-nation.
6. Scott Thuma,"Racial Diversity Increasing In U.S. Congregations," *HuffPost*, March 24, 2013, http://www.huffingtonpost.com/scott-thumma-phd/racial-diversity-increasing-in-us-congregations_b_2944470.html.

Chapter 3

1. "Andrew Young On 1996 Olympics: 'We Were Working Together,'" News WABE Station, July 21, 2016, http://news.wabe.org/post/andrew-young-1996-olympics-we-were-working-together.
2. Malcolm Gladwell, *Blink* (New York: Little, Brown and Company, 2005), 77.
3. Gladwell, *Blink*.
4. "Africa Calls for Slavery Apology," CNN.com/WORLD, September 1, 2001, http://www.cnn.com/2001/WORLD/africa/09/01/durban.slavery/.
5. "Africa Calls for Slavery Apology."
6. Henry Hanks, "Blindfolded Muslim Man Hugs Mourners in Paris," CNN, November 20, 2015, http://www.cnn.com/2015/11/19/world/muslim-man-hugs-paris-feat/.
7. Charles H. Spurgeon, *The Treasury of David—Volume 1 (Psalm 51).* (Peabody, MA: Hendrickson Publishers, 208), 402.
8. "David Wilkerson Quotes," BrainyQuotes.com, https://www.brainyquote.com/quotes/quotes/d/davidwilke296520.html.
9. William Douglas Chamberlain, *The Meaning of Repentance* (Philadelphia: Westminster Press, 1943), 23.
10. Oswald Chambers, *My Utmost for His Highest* (Grand Rapids, MI: Discovery House Publishers, 1989).

Chapter 4

1. Leon Morris, *The Gospel According to John*, The New International Commentary on the New Testament (Grand Rapids, MI: Eerdmans, 1971), 617.

2.   Kathleen Hopkins,"Teen gets 3 1/2 years in crash that killed best friend," *Asbury Park Press*, January 23, 2015, http://www.app.com/story/news/local/toms-river-area/toms-river/2015/01/23/conor-hanifin-sentenced-toms-river-crash-killed-best-friend/22225755/.
3.   Hopkins, "Teen gets 3 1/2 years in crash that killed best friend."
4.   Mark Berman, " 'I forgive you.' Relatives of Charleston church shooting victims address Dylann Roof," *The Washington Post*, June 19, 2015, https://www.washingtonpost.com/news/post-nation/wp/2015/06/19/i-forgive-you-relatives-of-charleston-church-victims-address-dylann-roof/?utm_term=.64cbebc6542d.

Chapter 5
1.   Libby Hill, "The Internet to Bill O'Reilly: Leave Congresswoman Maxine Waters' hair out of this," *Los Angeles Times*, March 28, 2017, http://www.latimes.com/entertainment/la-et-entertainment-news-updates-march-bill-o-reilly-uses-bully-pulpit-to-mock-1490728898-htmlstory.html.
2.   Shelby Steele, *A Dream Deferred* (San Francisco: Harper Collins, 1998), 146.
3.   *Random House College Dictionary*, Revised Edition, s.v. "tolerance."
4.   *English Living Oxford Dictionary*, online edition, s.v. "tolerance." https://en.oxforddictionaries.com/definition/tolerance.

Chapter 6
1.   Madeline Holcombe, "Black and white friends try to trick teacher with matching haircuts," CNN, March 3, 2017. http://www.cnn.com/2017/03/03/us/black-and-white-friends-haircut-trnd/.
2.   Scripture taken from *The Message*. Copyright © 1993, 1994, 1995, 1996, 2000, 2001, 2002. Used by permission of NavPress Publishing Group.
3.   CNN Wire Staff, "Rodney King dead at 47," June 18, 2012, http://www.cnn.com/2012/06/17/us/obit-rodney-king/.

Chapter 7
1.   Philip Schaff, *History of the Christian Church*, vol. 2 (Grand Rapids: William B. Eerdmans Publishing,1910), 146.
2.   Jim Jones, "Crusade: Latino Catholics Boost Graham Crusade Attendance," *Christianity Today*, May 19, 1997, http://www.christianitytoday.com/ct/1997/may19/7t6051.html.
3.   Jones, "Crusade."
4.   "Elie Wiesel Quotes," Wisdom Quotes, http://www.wisdomquotes.com/quote/elie-wiesel-7.html.
5.   Larry A. Samovar and Richard E. Porter, *Intercultural Communication* (Belmont, CA: Wadsworth Publishing, 1982), 23.

6. Sonja Haller, "'I Hurt with Her': Young friends comfort each other after racial slur," *All the Moms*, http://allthemoms. com/2017/08/17/i-hurt-with-her-young-friends-comfort-each-other-after-racial-slur/.

Chapter 8
1. David D. Ireland, "Minority Perspectives of Interracial Relationships in Large Multiracial Churches" (PhD diss., Regent University, 2002).
2. Vinson Synan, Ed. *Aspects of Pentecostal-Charismatic Origins* (Plainfield, NJ: Logos International, 1975), 11.
3. A. W. Tozer, *The Pursuit of God* (WLC, 2009), 12.

Chapter 9
1. L. L., Paglis and S. G. Greene, "Leadership Self-Efficacy and Managers' Motivation for Leading Change," in *Journal of Organizational Behavior* 23, (2002): 215–235.
2. Justo L. Gonzalez, *Out of Every Tribe & Nation: Christian Theology at the Ethnic Roundtable* (Nashville, TN: Abingdon Press, 1992), 83.
3. Gonzalez, *Out of Every Tribe & Nation*.
4. Miguel A. De La Torre and Edwin David Aponte, *Introducing Latino/a Theologies* (Maryknoll, NY: Orbis Books, 2001), 12.
5. Thomas Kochman, *Black and White Styles in Conflict* (Chicago, IL: The University of Chicago Press, 1981), 3.
6. Wesley E. Duewel, *Heroes of the Holy Life* (Grand Rapids, MI: Zondervan, 2002), 92.
7. Cambridge Dictionary, online edition, s.v. "radicalized."
8. James Ryle, "GRACE—God's Unspeakable Gift," Identity Network, http://www.identitynetwork.org/apps/articles/default. asp?articleid=71830&columnid=.
9. James S. Hewett, *Illustrations Unlimited: Topical Collection of Hundreds of Stories, Quotations and Humor for Speakers, Writers, Pastors and Teachers* (Wheaton, IL: Tyndale, 1988), 249.

Conclusion
1. Stanley W. Green, The Canadian Mennonite (9-4-00), p. 11; submitted by Herb Franz, Winkler, Manitoba, Canada © 2001 PreachingToday. com / Christianity Today, International.
2. "Hiroo Onoda, Japanese soldier who long refused to surrender, dies at 91," CNN, January 17, 2014, http://www.cnn.com/2014/01/17/world/asia/japan-philippines-ww2-soldier-dies/.

Index